Obscenity, Pornography, & Censorship

Perry C. Cotham

Baker Book House

Grand Rapids, Michigan

© 1973 by
Baker Book House Company

ISBN: 0-8010-2345-9

Printed in the United States of America

Acknowledgments

This book began almost inadvertently. In making plans to edit another book in the area of church and society, none of the writers I had contacted had wanted to assume an assignment on a Christian response to obscenity and pornography. I took it upon myself to write such a study and, having more research than I could use in a brief study, I decided to expand this chapter into a book. I am motivated by the belief that while too many conservative and fundamentalist Christians, and even ministers, have no lack of zeal over the topic, they do lack an adequate understanding of what pornography and obscenity is and what it does. I hope that this book can reach that audience.

This is submitted with a belief (typical to many writers, I am sure) that the writing and revision process is not complete but simply has to be terminated to meet a publisher's deadline. In my case, the regular professorial duties of the past calendar year have been complicated by the teaching of six new courses, three outside my major field; and these assignments, plus the "orientation" required with the arrival of a new baby into the family, have made great inroads into what little extra time was available.

The manuscript is submitted with some trepidation.

There is the fear (again known to many writers) that immediately after this appears in print I will change my mind about some line of analysis or major conclusion. To cite one example, I already suspect that an opinion expressed in Chapter 5 about the public satiation with purely pornographic films and "the pendulum swinging the other direction" might be easily refuted. The long lines that waited to pay handsomely to see *Deep Throat* in New York before a judge banned the film could be a solid piece of evidence for my critics.

Every source I used in research may be found listed in the documentation at the end of the chapters, so the reader may trace the mental gymnastics I went through in completing this study. I am indebted to these sources for many of my own ideas and interpretations.

My hope and prayer is that this book can be used to the glory of God and the betterment of humanity. Teaching in a Christian college has presented some disadvantages and uniquely interesting problems, but the overwhelming and gratifying value of affiliation with such an institution has been the initial stimulus and I have received the continual encouragement of young Christians to become involved in issues like this one (and others of much greater gravity) and devote time and energy to placing such issues in the context of genuine biblical morality. If the book were to be dedicated to anyone, it would be to my students.

Now, to be more specific. Making small but helpful contributions to the preparation of this volume are Nancy Gist, Joy Sanders, and my wife, Glenda. (In the case of the latter, I will avoid the temptation to elaborate on the point of her exercising the necessary patience while caring for three children and . . . etc., etc.)

More importantly, with deep appreciation I acknowl-

Pastor William Hoffman
308 N. Fairview Drive
Luverne,
Minnesota 56156

Obscenity, Pornography, & Censorship

edge the assistance of three others: Dr. Prentice A. Meador, Jr., Associate Professor of Speech at the University of Washington, for taking time from his own busy schedule of lecturing and writing books to read the manuscript and write a foreword. Also, Dr. Dennis Loyd, Associate Professor of English at David Lipscomb College, for reading the entire manuscript and making a number of valuable suggestions related to substance and style. Adding already to his distinction as a scholar, Dr. Loyd was once an expert witness in a Nashville pornography trial and most of his colleagues, including myself, refuse to let him forget this unique experience. And last but not least, Debbie Barnet, an underpaid and overworked student secretary for the summer of '72, for typing all of the first draft and several pages of revised material.

Perry C. Cotham
David Lipscomb College
Nashville, Tennessee 37203

April 6, 1973

Foreword

Thoughtful observers of national trends in America point out that these unsettled times may produce a powerful reaction. For example, Herman Kahn, who heads the Hudson Institute at Croton-on-Hudson, N.Y., suggests that such reactions in the past came "to increasingly educated, hedonistic, and secular societies that offended the spiritual and moral sensibilities of ordinary citizens." He believes that such is the case in America of the 1970's: many ordinary citizens are offended by pornography, permissiveness, increased tolerance concerning sex, and a lesser regard for more traditional values. Consequently, a "counterreformation" is underway in America according to Kahn (*The National Review*, March 10, 1973, p. 1). "The polls show," says Michael Novak, author of a new book on contemporary white ethnic groups in America, "that the hard-hat construction workers on Wall Street were more opposed to the war than other occupational groups, including brokers and doctors. But when the long-haired kids came around spitting on the flag and shouting obscenities, that was too much. The hard hats struck" (*The National Review*, March 10, 1973, p. 16).

The hard hats reacted in part to the obscene language spoken freely in the wide open spaces of the public.

Such language is perceived as a thread in an ever larger fabric of obscenities—X-rated films, blue theatre, topless bars, and radio and TV violence. An author who wants to speak to today's world about these things and at the same time steer a safe course must speak cautiously and avoid controversial questions. This might seem doubly true for a person who holds Christian values.

But Perry Cotham will have no part of a sheltered Christianity spoken in quiet remote corners on questions no one is asking. In this book he prefers to lay out his perspective on pornography, obscenity, and censorship in clear, unmistakable terms, unprotected by all the qualifications usually found in specialized publications for limited audiences. He does so from the point of view of a concerned Christian and his view is rooted and grounded in a Biblical theology of man, his nature, his potential, and his responsibilities. Although his blunt language may lose some technical, scientific specificity, most readers will understand what he means and will probably prefer his version. No doubt all Christians will appreciate Cotham realistically bringing the Christian perspective to vital issues of pornography, obscenity, and censorship.

Obscenity, Pornography, and Censorship: A Christian Perspective contains a significant amount of information, analysis, and wisdom. In large part, it is a cultural critique of our society and our world—attempts to dehumanize people, to quantify persons, to violate the personhood of individual men and women by seeing them as less than persons. In part, it is a theological critique of the media, advertising, language, violence, real life written by a Christian to uphold the worth and dignity of the individual. Inevitably, not all the conclusions will be accepted by all readers, whether Christians or not. In reading the original manuscript, I found myself tempted to enter marginal notes, but in the end, I decided that my notes would probably add little to the major import of this manuscript.

I especially appreciate that Cotham has not tried to approach these tough areas from a "value-free" viewpoint. He does care that the Christian perspective be brought to bear on pornography and obscenity. For instance, it is apparent that he does stand against pornography and obscenity, that he does respect responsible freedom of individuals, and that he does believe the church should bring a positive witness to the whole subject.

I consider it a privilege to introduce you to this work and I hope that the values it speaks will prevail in our times.

Prentice A. Meador, Jr.

Seattle, Washington

Table of Contents

1

Introduction

Check one of the two following propositions:

☐ Crisis-stricken America is on the verge of a total moral and spiritual collapse. Certainly Sodom and Gomorrah or the Roman empire before her fall could not have been as morally corrupted as America in the 1970's. The assinine decisions of the spineless Supreme Court have, in the name of freedom, granted total permissiveness to novelists, film producers, playwrights, and entertainers, and this has produced a society teeming with depraved smut peddlers concerned only with the almighty dollar. The standards that guided us to greatness have been undermined by this new license, and the moral principles of our youth have been so subverted that it is only a matter of time before this great nation falls into the hands of the Communists or other godless dictators.

* * *

☐ Owing to the progressive decisions of the American court system and the changing attitudes of the younger generation, America is now in a position to enjoy and profit by the freedoms and opportunities made possible by a long overdue sexual revolution. No longer restricted by the vestiges of hypocritical Victorian prudery, each mature citizen is now free to choose for himself what he wants to see or read or do and artists of the media now enjoy the legal sanction necessary to insure that citizen of a wide variety of choices. This long lost freedom has already brought our society, especially among the youth, to a more honest, sensitive, and humane approach to interpersonal relations.

* * *

☐ Check here if you believe that neither of the above views is truly accurate and on a separate sheet of paper submit your own statement in a hundred words or less.

* * *

There has been no lack of doctrinaires in the continuing discussion of pornography and obscenity. Then why another study of this matter? Standing in a tradition of sermons, lectures, religious articles, and parental warnings, surely we Christians know where we stand on this issue. We're unequivocally and irrevocably opposed to pornography and obscenity, aren't we? It seems that we are not so certain!

The point of the little beginning exercise should be evident—the issue of morality in media is so complex and confusing that it defies easy answers. Because it is human nature to seek simple causes and solutions to complicated problems, either polar position is relatively easy to understand. Advocates of total freedom in expression point to the right of free speech guaranteed by the First Amendment and can cite a long list of decisions embarassing to self-appointed do-gooders who censored worthwhile material to substantiate the claim that limitations on that amendment are questionable at best and dangerous at worst. At the other end of the spectrum are those who, aware of the influence of the media in public morality, would have the government at all levels impose a strict censorship over public sexual expression and, possibly but not necessarily, over other areas of expression that degrade human dignity.

But what should be the Christian's response to the problems of pornography and obscenity? Can he know what is obscene and pornographic? Should he work to impose his standards on the remainder of society? In selecting our own books, magazines, movies, and places of entertainment, where should we draw the line? Are there special guidelines needed by Christian artists to be applied in their communicative efforts? For that matter, is the issue really all that important? Can Christians dare to be at ease with the Congressional Commission on Obscenity and Pornography finding that only 2 percent of our populace placed concern over erotic materials among "the two or three most serious problems facing the country today"?

These are the questions with which this study will deal. At the outset one thing needs saying. This topic can be approached from several perspectives. The approach here is not from that of a psychologist, psychiatrist, or other social scientist, but of a concerned Christian layman. It is rooted in the biblical theology of the doctrine of man and human society. But this approach cannot be indifferent, and certainly not antagonistic, to the insight and discoveries offered by students of this topic in other fields of inquiry. Christian social ethics should be interdisciplinary in nature, requiring its students to undertake joint and complementary theoretical and empirical studies in theology, philosophical ethics, and historical and behavioral sciences. It is in that spirit that I shall proceed.

2

Dimensions of the Problem

We begin by acknowledging cause for concern. Who would question the assertion that our society is significantly different from the one in which our parents and grandparents lived? The growing climate of permissiveness and, perhaps as much as any other factor, the Pill, have given Americans more sexual freedom than any previous generation. The debate over the breadth and depth of real change in today's sexual behavior patterns will be left to the sociologists and theologians. The most spectacular and the easiest identifiable changes are in what we may see, hear, and read, and in this respect America is by far one of the freest nations in the Western world. Perhaps most noteworthy of all, citizens who formerly rose up in united, puritanical wrath whenever any private part was placed before public gaze now seem, on the whole, to be taking the boom in commercialized prurience in stride with considerable nonchalance.

MOTION PICTURES

These changes are most conspicuous in the entertaining arts. In the twentieth century movies have reigned as one of the primary recreational outlets for Americans.

No medium has gained ascendancy as king of the entertaining arts quite like the film. This year box office receipts from some 14,000 theatres will come to slightly over one billion dollars; it is estimated that 20 million persons attend motion pictures weekly. Add to this the fact that millions will see movies in their homes via television and the role of the film kingdom as a great global educator is enhanced.

It is true that, despite considerably higher ticket prices, movie admissions represent a declining percentage of total American expenditures. Whereas Americans spent 80 percent of their amusement dollar on movies in 1947, 68 percent in 1957, they now spend a little less than 50 percent.[1] But the most important statistics are those showing that the movie industry depends largely upon the youth for its support. A study by the Opinion Research Corporation discovered that the vast majority of moviegoers are under thirty, more than half are under twenty, and almost a third are under fifteen.[2]

American movie fans have been given glimpses of the bodies of their stars (under varying shooting angles, distance, color, and lighting) ever since Theda Bara bared her breasts in 1917 in *Cleopatra.* But motion pictures generally have never enjoyed the breadth of freedom granted the printed media and for over half a century censorship was tolerated and seldom challenged in view of the operation of official movie censorship boards in a number of states and municipalities. Striving to maintain and expand the mass market, major producers were much more interested in giving movie buffs

1. William L. Rivers, Theodore Peterson, Jay W. Jensen, *The Mass Media and Modern Society* (San Francisco: Rinehart Press, 1971), pp. 280-81.
2. *Ibid.*

what they wanted rather than championing the right to dissent.

Hardly an eyebrow would be raised today, but when Howard Hughes' discovery, a nineteen-year-old named Jane Russell hiked her skirt, loosened her blouse, and stretched in a haystack for a love scene in *The Outlaw* in 1941, it created a protracted furor in Hollywood. The Legion of Decency condemned it and Hollywood's Johnston office refused to bestow its approval until 103 cuts were made and the promotional ads showing "a man and a woman together in a compromising horizontal position" were scrapped.[3] Hughes delayed release of the film until 1946. Things were soon to change.

In the early fifties McCarthyism was rampant and blacklists of suspected Communists among actors, writers, and directors were in wide circulation. When McCarthyism had subsided in the late fifties, major producers who dared to challenge such agencies as the National Legion of Decency with films like *Never on Sunday* and *Room at the Top* learned that seals of approval had become an anachronism. Concomitantly, "art theatres" exhibited foreign films that treated sexual matters with a degree of explicitness not found in general release films of the same decade.

About 1966 the film producers waxed bolder and bolder in testing the limits of decency. That year Italian director Michelangelo Antonioni broke the taboo against head-on, total nudity in *Blow-Up*. The controversial sequence was brief but the precedent for first-run films was established and the movie was a harbinger of the candor to come. Popular films that would have been cut or even confiscated by authorities in the early sixties

---

3. *Newsweek*, November 13, 1967, p. 22.

for their sexual explicitness include *The Graduate, Midnight Cowboy, Romeo and Juliet, M*A*S*H, Catch-22, Ryan's Daughter, Summer of '42, Carnal Knowledge, The Last Picture Show, A Clockwork Orange, Portnoy's Complaint,* and *Last Tango in Paris.*

Language has also taken a much earthier tone since 1966. It was that year that Edward Albee's *Who's Afraid of Virginia Woolf?* appeared on the screen and stirred wide controversy.[4] The realistic dialogue included "Jesus" or "Christ" used irreverently seventeen times and the name of God was employed in curse expressions forty-four times, not to mention numerous other expressions and epithets previously excluded from sound tracks. There is probably not a single word or expression that could not be uttered in general films today. How far we have come from 1953 when Hollywood refused to sanction Otto Preminger's *The Moon is Blue* because of the word "virgin"! Was it only a generation ago that Clark Gable's immortal line in *Gone With the Wind,* "Frankly, my dear, I don't give a damn" caused an outcry of the public's righteous indignation?

Today there is not a single major area of sexual conduct which has not been the central subject, with serious treatment or otherwise, of widely distributed general release films. Homosexuality for both sexes lost much of its stigma in films like *The Fox, The Killing of Sister George, The Boys in the Band,* and *Deliverance.* Mate-swapping received its first major treatment with

---

4. For a report of this controversy, see the cover story of *Life,* June 10, 1966, pp. 87-89. Who would have imagined in 1966 that this movie would be beamed into homes all across America via prime-time network television? And yet, on February 22, 1973, on CBS Thursday Night at the Movies, the movie was shown with very little editing and, apparently, very little complaint.

Bob & Carol & Ted & Alice. Fellatio was depicted in *Catch-22* and miscegenation, another former taboo, was taken in stride when it cropped up in *The Liberation of L. B. Jones* and *Getting Straight.* Concubinage with a special twist was treated in *The Baby Maker.* "Sex reassignment" was treated in a semi-documentary, *The Christine Jorgenson Story.* Voyeurism was the chief theme of *Marriage of a Young Stockbroker* and the themes of *The Married Priest* and *The Priest's Wife* should be evident. Masturbation and most other aspects of sex are treated in *Portnoy's Complaint,* a film version of Philip Roth's best-selling novel.

The rest of this chapter could be filled with numerous films which have treated promiscuity, fornication, adultery, prostitution, and abortion. These themes are not new to moviegoers but in an earlier era they had to be treated implicitly and often with the requirement of a plot revealing "just retribution" for the sexual misdeeds of the principals.

The new freedom was made possible in large measure by the initiation in 1968 of the rating system by Jack Valenti's Motion Picture Association of America. The rating system has been generally acceptable to the public but many responsible critics inside and outside the industry perceived inconsistency in criteria and self-serving hypocrisy in the self-appointed guardianship. Moviemakers were aware that X-rated films no longer were respected in many quarters; indeed some newspapers no longer accepted advertisement for X films and there was growing support for major companies abandoning such films altogether. As the months passed, more and more explicitness was allowed in each main category[5] and in

---

5. Note that *The Graduate* has moved from an X rating to PG in 1972. A couple of cuts were made in the fall of 1972 on *A*

May, 1971, the rating system lost the support of both the National Council of Churches (Protestant) and the National Catholic Office for Motion Pictures. There was a time when various European imports, often presented to the courts and the public under the guise of being sex documentaries,[6] were more popular among voyeurs than American productions. This is no longer true.

"SEXPLOITATION" FILMS

The new freedom experienced by straight commercial films has forced the "underground" and "sexploitation" movies to unimaginable lows in explicitness and aesthetics in order to pioneer in the novel and unique. In the early seventies, according to *Time*, full-length feature "porno" films continued to make up by far the most profitable and fastest growing segment of the pornography business.[7] Two-bit peep show machines, the grainy amateur films featuring aging or second-class strippers, have been replaced by slick color productions with sound, narratives, and attractive young models hoping to earn money for university tuition or be discovered by major producers. These movies, offered under such titles as *Man and Wife* (this film cost $32,000 to produce and grossed over $4,500,000), *Zodiac Couples, The Post-Graduate, The History of the Blue Movie,The Steward-esses*, appear in downtown movie houses across the country.

Clockwork Orange to bring that movie from an X rating to R. *Time*, September 11, 1972, p. 68.
6. Films like *Censorship in Denmark*, the Kronhausens' *Freedom to Love, Pornography: Copenhagen 1970, Sexual Freedom in Denmark, Famous Homosexuals of History*, and *The Flanders and Alcott Report on Sex Response*.
7. *Time*, November 16, 1970, p. 92; see also *Newsweek*, December 21, 1970, pp. 26-28.

In 1973 one of these purely pornographic films became a *cause célèbre*. The movie *Deep Throat* was probably not much more or much less prurient than a score of similar films available at the same time to the public, except that it had attracted long lines of middle-class customers waiting to be titillated, and it grossed well over one million dollars at Manhattan's World Theatre alone. The main theme of the film was oral sex; in a span of seventy minutes it depicted fifteen overt acts, including seven of fellatio and four of cunnilingus. The film was approved by a jury in Binghamton, New York, but was later halted by a New York judge, Criminal Court Judge Joel J. Taylor. In testimony, *Saturday Review* critic Arthur Knight praised the film for acknowledging "the importance of female sexual gratification." Apparently psychoanalyst and professor of sociology Ernest Van den Haag felt there were better ways to acknowledge this reality. Calling the film "a transparent pretext for showing sexual scenes," Van den Haag told the court that a pervasive social attitude that condones treating bodies purely as a means of pleasure, without regard for their humanity, constitutes a real social danger.[8] The judge agreed, calling the film a "feast of carrion and squalor," "a nadir of decadence," and "a Sodom and Gomorrah gone wild before the fire."[9]

The words Judge Taylor used in describing *Deep Throat* could apply to many other films of this genre and not be verbal overkill. Nothing is held back— nothing except taste. Any and everything that some human mind can fantasize sexually seems to be appro-

8. *Newsweek*, January 15, 1973, p. 50; see also *Time*, January 15, 1973, p. 46.
9. *Newsweek*, March 12, 1973, p. 22.

priate for such films—girls copulating with horses and pigs, views of sexually connected couples, and often groups, of both sexes or the same sex gyrating to music, and the zoom lens of the camera probing every slimy pore, recess, and hair in the pink and white tissue of male and female genitalia. One journalist commented that such exploitation films were reminiscent of and, for the regular voyeur, probably about as exciting as open-heart surgery. The films are largely made by the young set and are viewed by their parents' generation. The police occasionally make arrests but in the face of public apathy and the difficulty of winning a court conviction their hearts do not seem to be in it.

Competition among these theatres has increased. Once charging five or six dollars for admission, competition has brought lower prices with further discounts for heterosexual couples and free admission for unescorted women. One Los Angeles theatre offers "six hours of continuous hard-core adult erotica." Another offers free popcorn and still another touts free coffee and sandwiches for the more faithful and indefatigable customers. Air conditioning, carpeting, and plush seating is a must for the more competitive houses.

The practical consequence of this new freedom is that the lines of demarcation between such "skin flicks" and general release films, once quite clear, is becoming increasingly difficult to draw. The situation became complicated in 1970 when a long-honored company, Twentieth Century-Fox, contracted professed pornographer Russ Meyer, thus providing him with the heavy financing and "respectability" to produce in *Beyond the Valley of the Dolls* a first-class exploitation film. There have been many since. And the most controversial of them all has been Bernardo Bertolucci's *Last Tango in*

Paris, starring Marlon Brando. "For boldness and brutality," states *Time,* "the intimate scenes are unprecedented in feature films." Whether the general public considered the film art or pornography, advance reservation sales and publicity had already guaranteed the film's financial success.[10]

THEATRE

For a long time, the theatre trailed far behind the cinema in the realistic portrayal of sex. Full nudity came to Broadway in 1968 in the smash musical *Hair.* The show attracted little attention when it opened but soon word of its celebrated and now relatively unremarkable nude scene at the conclusion of the first act brought a stampede of ticket buyers. The obvious message and merit of *Hair* made possible opportunities for its staging in practically all of the major cities of the United States and Western world, and this has brought greater acceptability or at least indifference to such scenes in other performances.

Some kind of a dubious landmark in erotic realism was set in 1969 with the off-off-Broadway production of *Che!* which featured, among other things, an ape raping a nun and several instances of simulated coitus. The police closed the show after the second performance and proceeded to jail the entire cast on charges of public lewdness and sodomy. A few weeks later the theatre reached yet another apogee with the opening of Kenneth Tynan's *Oh! Calcutta!,* a revue billed as "ele-

---

10. Cover stories with scenes from the movie appeared in *Time,* January 22, 1973, pp. 51-55 and *Newsweek,* February 12, 1973, pp. 54-57.

gant eroticism." Staged in an old burlesque house wistfully renamed "Eden," the show is performed almost entirely in the nude and includes various sketches of mass masturbation, rape, mate-swapping, and other forms of sexuality. Many responsible critics called the production both anti-erotic and a sheer bore but month after month long lines of ticket seekers waited to pay as much as $25 for admission and the production was piped into many major U.S. cities via closed circuit television.

A number of so-called "dirty shows" opened in New York in the late sixties and early seventies. In fact one was entitled *The Dirtiest Show in Town* but it may be questioned whether it lived up to its name. This evoked the outrage of well-known Broadway producer David Merrick, who said:

> Hard-core pornography is nothing new, but rarely in modern history has this kind of material paraded as legitimate theater. Now, for the price of a Broadway ticket, the audience may be lured into a converted garage or loft, seated on wooden chairs and, in an atmosphere redolent of a gymnasium, watch a stage full of zombies mime sexual acts without reference to love or affection or joy. It is mechanical performing, and therefore not even lewd. It is no turn-on. It is a bore.
>
> I am concerned about this because live theater, while small compared to some of the other arts, is wide in influence. It is a seedbed of our culture. The theater translates many important novels into the spoken word; we pass on to the movies our visions, the fruits of our talent. What we do in the theater affects

texture of our society, influences the moral and, yes, political attitudes of our nation.[11]

TELEVISION

It has been quipped that of all the peoples of the earth, Americans, with their millions of radio and television sets, apparently stand most in fear of a moment of silence. By 1970, 95% of American homes owned at least one television set and 30% of the households had two or more sets. According to the A. C. Nielsen Company, these sets are being viewed about six hours a day in each home.[12] With its permeation of everyday life in America, we are just beginning to understand something of its gigantic impact in creating culture, affecting tastes in all forms of entertainment, creating demand for products and services, altering staid political processes, changing social habits and creating new ones, and providing each viewer with a roving eye and ear to history in the making. We are dealing with what someone has appropriately called the "massest medium."

Because of its easy accessibility to all groups and all ages, television has generally been the most conservative and reactionary of all mass media. But in the last six or seven years television has been experiencing its own mini-revolution in terms of language employed, explicit violence, and candor in the treatment of sexual themes, many of which were not even alluded to in the early

11. David Merrick, "Must Smut Smother the Stage?" *Reader's Digest*, March, 1970, p. 104.
12. Giraud Chester, Garnet R. Garrison, and Edgar E. Willis, *Television and Radio* (4th ed. rev.; New York: Appleton-Century-Crofts, 1971), p. 5. See also Sydney W. Head, *Broadcasting in America* (2nd ed. rev.; Boston: Houghton Mifflin Co., 1972), pp. 1-19.

days of the medium. For example, the most popular show of the 1971-72 season, *All in the Family*, aired on Saturday evening prime time, dealt with such themes as menopause, impotency, adultery, bigotry, and other themes with occasional sprinklings of traditional profanity. Movies exhibited in theatres a few years earlier brought new explicitness to the living rooms and dens of millions when aired over television. Some scenes and language were expurgated from many of the films but there has been a backlash of outrage from many viewers claiming some of these films should never have been considered appropriate for television audiences. A kind of mini-landmark was passed in the fall of 1972 with the network showing of the made-for-television movie *A Certain Summer*. The film dealt directly with the problem of a homosexual father and how he attempted to communicate the frustrations and despair of such a problem to his teen-age son. The story was very tastefully and maturely told, but some local stations, fearing vocal disapproval, opted for videotaping the movie and broadcasting it in the late evening and early morning hours. The show substituted in prime time for our city was, ironically, filled with violence.

It is fair to ask about the direction of television for the future. If the pattern of programming in other English speaking nations is followed, there will be more explicitness in treating sexual content. British television, long censorious in showing violence, has been much freer in treating sex and the human body. In March, 1972, Sydney, Australia, viewers were offered a show entitled *No. 96*, "a kind of salacious *Peyton Place*" which chronicled the escapades and predicaments of the swinging apartment dwellers of Sydney's Paddington district. Frequent glimpses of nude backsides and partial frontal nudity have caused the program to rise to the top of the ratings. The motivation for the daily series was made clear by co-producer Don Cash: "We're not making great television. We were asked by a commercial TV station to produce a program that appeals to a mass market and makes money. That is all we set out to do."[13] The success among Australian audiences has led the creators to look for export markets.

In America the Public Broadcasting System has been making small and quiet contributions to the revolution. Set in classical productions imported from England have been fleeting glimpses of nudity that were integral parts of the plot.[14] The three American commercial networks have never shown a nude scene, although nudity is often implied. Commenting on this trend, Robert D. Wood, president of the CBS Television network, said, "I wouldn't say that nudity will never come to commercial television. It's like football. It's a game of inches. We may get to where the BBC is now in seven or eight years."[15]

In April, 1973, the Federal Communications Commission announced an unprecedented inquiry into sex on the airwaves. The commission noted that in recent months some 3,000 complaints about allegedly obscene programming had been filed and hearings were planned to investigate the charges. There have been two major complaints. First, cable television, designed to provide clearer reception in rural communities and urban apartments, has offered its viewers in some cities late night

13. *Time*, June 5, 1972, p. 62.
14. These shows include *Jude the Obscure* in the "Masterpiece Theatre" Series, *The Triumph of Christy Brown*, and *Cold Comfort Farm*.
15. *Nashville Tennessean*, December 12, 1971.

"adult" film festivals that occasionally present X-rated fare. Apparently there have been no holds barred on some of the new "public access" channels and the stir gave rise to a vigilance group called Concerned Citizens on Public Access.[16] Another recent innovation that has drawn widespread complaint is the radio sex-talk programs that began in San Francisco and Los Angeles ("X-rated" radio). These are call-in talk shows featuring rap sessions between hosts and listeners on all manner of sexual subjects. [17] Of course serious sex information has long been needed but these shows are centered around questions designed more for entertainment (Sample: "Where did you have your most exciting affair?") and audience ratings with concomitant revenue than public enlightenment.

THE PRINTED MEDIA

In another area, the serious reader of literature will find that the changes in literary art have not been so rapid or profound as in the movies or theatre. The long and interesting history of how various books appeared on the scene soon to be banned in certain parts of the country and later winning court battles and eventually public acceptance as works of measurable merit will not be detailed here.[18] But we should note some landmark cases.

---

16. *Newsweek*, April 9, 1973, p. 83.
17. *Newsweek*, September 4, 1972, p. 90.
18. If the reader is interested in more information in this area, the following volume is recommended: Morris L. Ernst and Alan U. Schwartz, *Censorship: The Search for the Obscene* (New York: Macmillan Co., 1964), a valuable work for those wishing to explore the many legal ramifications of obscenity. Adding to its value are the many quotations from statute books and judicial opinions.

Going back a century, a significant and long-standing Victorian ruling on obscenity was in *Queen v. Hicklin* (1868). The question for decision was: If it be acknowledged that a book is obscene and its publication likely to prejudice good morals, is such publication lawful because the publisher's object was a lawful one? The court answered no. But it was not the court's decision that made the case important but the opinion of Lord Chief Justice Cockburn delivered *obiter dictum* (i.e., not binding as law). Cockburn gave an opinion of what obscenity is which was to be reprinted in textbooks and cited as the authoritative criterion by which allegations of obscenity were judged. The criterion: "Whether the tendency of the matter charged as obscenity is to deprave and corrupt those whose minds are open to such immoral influences and into whose hands a publication of this sort may fall." So a book was obscene if it had isolated passages which might adversely affect especially susceptible persons.[19] Practically speaking, this definition applied consistently would have reduced literature to the level of nursery rhymes.

English common law as it had evolved at the time of the Revolution was carried over into American law. The sensitivity of American judges, and particularly the federal judges, to English legal opinion caused the American courts to follow English judicial developments on this and other matters very closely. American judges readily turned to the Cockburn criterion in handling obscenity cases. Stiffer laws led to literary "smut-hunting," and it may seem incredible that Walt Whitman's *Leaves of Grass* was banned at one time. In the latter

---

19. See a discussion of this case in Alec Craig, *Suppressed Books: A History of the Conception of Literary Censorship* (Cleveland: World Publishing Company, 1963), pp. 40-53.

nineteenth century, Anthony Comstock appeared on the American scene. To Comstock, anything that savored of sex was obscene. He started his career in New York by making arrests under a state act dealing with obscenity; by 1872 he was working for the Y.M.C.A., which had established a Committee for the Suppression of Vice. The following year he managed to get through Congress a comprehensive bill, known as the Comstock Act, which stiffened the federal law dealing with obscene publications, including information about contraception. Comstockery did not end with his death in 1915. Prior to 1930, Massachusetts courts had convicted booksellers of peddling some of the works of Upton Sinclair, H. G. Wells, Sinclair Lewis (*Elmer Gantry*), D. H. Lawrence (*Lady Chatterley's Lover*, naturally), and Ernest Hemingway (*The Sun Also Rises*).

The tide took a dramatic turn against Comstockery in 1933. This was the year of the *Ulysses* case, the first major case that broke with *Queen v. Hicklin* (1868). James Joyce's novel, long circulated clandestinely, became legally available when Judge Woolsey admitted that the long-banned *Ulysses* was unusually frank, but he did not find the "leer of the sensualist" present nor that the book was "dirt for dirt's sake." The book might have a "somewhat emetic" effect on the reader, but "nowhere does it tend to be aphrodisiac." It was a "sincere and honest book" and must be judged as such.[20] Woolsey put emphasis on the author's intent and the book's "dominant effect."

Then in 1957 the Supreme Court in the Roth case made its first serious effort to grapple with the problem of obscenity and the First Amendment. Ironically, this

20. For the complete text of Judge Woolsey's opinion, see the Appendix in *ibid*, pp. 218-22.

pivotal Supreme Court decision upheld the conviction of Roth for mailing indecent books, but at the same time firmly established new and more liberal obscenity criteria, to which we will refer in the next chapter. Then in 1964, Henry Miller's *Tropic of Cancer*, perhaps the most litigated book in the history of literature, passed a Supreme Court test.

The earliest American obscenity case dates back to 1821, when a pornographic eighteenth century novel about a prostitute, popularly known as Fanny Hill, was suppressed. But in 1966, the Supreme Court lifted the ban by a vote of 6 to 3, finding the book had some redeeming social value after all. On the same day the Court handed down decisions against *Eros* and other publications of Ralph Ginzburg, who sought to expand sales by luridly suggestive advertising which the Court took as evidence of the publisher's intent to appeal to the reader's prurient interests (Ginzburg was released from serving a prison term in late 1972). Also a decision was handed down against Edward Mishkin's hard-core pornography. Altogether the justices wrote fourteen different opinions on these three cases—a symptom of the continuing difficulty of reaching agreement on obscenity issues. But 1966 was the year that, for all practical purposes, literary censorship was ended.[21]

The emerging problem that now demands attention is the fact that the line between works that possess genuine literary merit and those that are predominantly pornographic becomes increasingly difficult to draw. And what do you do with a book that is an interesting

---

21. For an in-depth discussion of the trials of *Lady Chatterley's Lover*, *Tropic of Cancer*, and *Fanny Hill* by the lawyer who defended them, see Charles Rembar, *The End of Obscenity* (New York: Random House, 1968).

mixture of the two ingredients (I refer, for example, to a book like Philip Roth's *The Breast*)? And, in too many cases, books enter the best seller lists distinguished only by the fact that once they would have placed their publishers in jail.

The unprecedented freedom enjoyed by serious novelists would seem a natural antidote to the proliferation of hard-core pornography. This has not been the case in recent years. Many Christians have followed with understandable alarm the increasing torrents of pornography flooding city newstands, candy and tobacco shops, even some drug stores, and advertising materials in the mails.[22] Smutty books and filthy pictures that were formerly the exclusive preserve of a few big-city merchants are now accessible from coast to coast, usually in downtown shops with alluring signs and window displays.

Of concern is the relative ease with which young people can purchase at outrageous prices (often from $3.50 to $6.00) magazines featuring large color photographs of male and female genitalia in exaggerated and titillating postures for maximum exposure, and paperback books (costing no more than 25¢ to produce and sold for $2.00 or more) that rely heavily on every conceivable profane and gutter term to describe in minute and lurid detail any form of hetero- and homosexual aberration. Usually the materials are segregated in display according to heterosexual or homosexual tastes. Many porno shops offer peep shows, three-sided booths

22. Pornography through the mails, or advertising for same, is often not considered a serious problem but over 230,000 protests over unsolicited pornography were reported to the Post Office in 1968. See *Newsweek*, October 6, 1969, p. 82. This has brought some protective legislation that has curbed the problem to some extent.

where flickering, blurry films (sometimes complete with sound) are shown at the drop of a quarter. On view inside the glass counter is a wide assortment of devices offered the adult—vibrators, French ticklers, costumes, films, artificial male and female organs—all sold as "novelties" which appeal to every kind of sex fantasy.

Sex tabloids have also been cashing in on "the rich pornocopia." The genre's prototype, *Screw*, was started in November, 1968, by two young journalists with a $350 investment that grossed $650,000 in the first year of operation. Tabloids like *Kiss, New York Review of Sex*, and *Pleasure* offer an underground-type mixture of smut and satire and their popularity has challenged the market of older tabloids such as *National Mirror* and the *National Enquirer* which rely on the blood-curdling sex and sadism formula. [23]

The proliferation of all this pornography has led dollar-hungry promoters to seek new means of keeping victims of erotic overkill in the fold. The latest innovation for smut buffs is the live sex show, in which a naked couple perform before viewers who may pay up to $15.00 to watch. Sometimes the features are centered around short plays about betrayal and reconciliation or classical interpretive dance routines (euphemistically called "the love dance") that culminate in slow, graceful intercourse, simulated or real. Such shows have been generally limited to New York, Los Angeles, and

---

23. See *Time*, November 16, 1970, p. 92, *Newsweek*, July 14, 1960, p. 80, and Maisie Ward, "Speaking of Sex . . . and so forth," *America*, June 12, 1971. In his column, Pete Hamill stated that "*Screw* and *Kiss* and their 40-odd imitators share newsstand space with the radical press: some radical papers have been forced to print an array of breasts and buttocks just to get the other material looked at, if not read." *New York Post*, July 13, 1970.

San Francisco, but most major American cities offer topless bars and discotheques as well as other types of variation on the titillation scene. For example, several clubs have amateur strip contests, massage parlors are cropping up as a new innovation, there was once a topless shoeshine at $2.00 a pair in Miami, visitors to Miami Beach for both political conventions in 1972 could "rent a girl" from several agencies (such as Supergirl, Inc., Sunshine Girls, Inc., and Rent-a-Bird) for a special date,[24] and at Detroit's Wayne State University, co-eds could earn tuition money by modeling nude for customers who wanted custom-made, do-it-yourself pornography with rented cameras or body paint.[25] What possible variation is still available to interest the clientele?

One thing modern day pornographers cannot be accused of is hypocrisy. An article appearing in *Newsweek* entitled "Sexploitation: Sin's Wages," pointed out that smut peddlers are otherwise respectable men who admit they are in business solely to make money. "What I'm doing is the American way," one exclaimed. "I'm capitalizing on this market and moving into more respected areas. I have a shoe store and I have invested in a new magazine." New York City and the west coast are the most profitable areas. In New York the number of massage parlors rose from 4 to 76 from 1971 to 1973.

---

24. *Nashville Tennessean*, July 6, 1972, told the story of Miami "Girl-for-hire" agencies. All three operations featured require customers to sign behavior agreements and all three contend they have firm rules against prostitution-type activities by employees.
25. See "Working Through College in the Nude," *Time*, December 13, 1971, p. 16. The models are identified only by number, one indication of the depersonalization such activity brings, a point to be discussed later.

The average porno bookstore can operate for $6,500 a month but takes in more than $31,000 a month. The film *Deep Throat* grossed $77,000 in one week. Pornographic publishing houses have turned out as many as forty new titles a month. The entire pornography business is now worth up to $800 million a year.[26] Can the tide ever be turned?

WHICH WAY MEDIA?

Frustration is bad enough, but sometimes the real disasters in life only begin when you get what you want. In the last several generations, a good number of intelligent and articulate individuals, generally called intellectual and/or liberal, have reasoned persuasively for total freedom in the arts and entertainment media. And within the past decade or so, the courts and legislatures have appraised these arguments as persuasive and have so acted (or failed to act, depending on one's view) that today, to all intents and purposes, governmental censorship has ceased to exist in the western world. We have what we've wanted.

Is there a sense of triumphant jubilation across the land? Hardly! There is, on the contrary, a growing uncertainty and apprehensiveness. We've gotten more than we bargained for and feel that basic liberty has been taken advantage of. Several notable civil libertarians have gone on record as asserting this is not what they meant at all. Morris Ernst, long-time opponent of censorship, declared he would not choose "to live in a society without limits to freedom." The lawyer who defended *Ulysses* continued:

---

26. *Newsweek*, February 12, 1973, pp. 78-79.

Whereas I defended the book and legitimatized a four letter word, that doesn't mean that the four letter word, out of context, should be spread and used—or sodomy on the stage or masturbation in the public arena here and the world over ... I deeply resent the idea that the lowest common denominator, the most tawdry magazine, pandering for profit, to use the Supreme Court word, should be able to compete in the marketplace with no restraints.[27]

Today we are continually and persistently bombarded with invitations from the media to participate voyeuristically in the sex lives of others, ideal or not, to be aroused, intimidated, and/or made guilty by that portrayal, and to preoccupy ourselves as sexual athletes with our own betterment through any one of the scores of quick, sure cures that proliferate today as wonder diets used to do. Rapidly approaching a *seductio ad absurdum,* America has inadvertently become a nation of 210 million involuntary peeping toms. A visitor from outer space who had time to study only our contemporary art and entertainment would return with an eccentric view of our reproductive process on earth.

In surveying the dimensions of this issue, mainly as it exists in the United States, we have attempted to avoid concrete judgments upon the effects of this freedom and commentary on the healthiness or lack of same in contemporary society. Disagreeable and repulsive as so many manifestations of new freedom may be, Christians must ask how much it really matters. Christians need to

---

27. *New York Times,* January 5, 1970, p. 46.

know the effects of pornography and obscenity on individuals and society as a whole before an appropriate response can be made. And if we are going to engage in a battle on this front, it is imperative that we know our enemy.

QUESTIONS FOR DISCUSSION

1. Is the sex morality of today's youth significantly different from yesteryear or are we just more open and frank in discussing sexual matters?
2. Can you think of films that seemed shockingly candid when you first saw them in a theatre but now seem very mild or have even been shown on television?
3. Do you think the movie rating code has enhanced or lowered the overall quality of general release films or is there little difference?
4. What would motivate people to pay five or six dollars to see a film that is totally pornographic and void of social and moral redeeming value?
5. Is it possible for a movie to depict nudity and sexual immorality while presenting a message that is morally good and positive?
6. Do you believe that opera, dramatic plays, and other forms of staged productions started using nudity and more explicitness in language merely to compete with motion pictures in this area?
7. Do you think that censors like Anthony Comstock are totally sincere or are publicity seekers on some kind of an "ego-trip"? Could it be they have unresolved sexual conflicts of their own?

3

Pinpointing the Problem:
What is Pornography and Obscenity?

The conservative distaste for pornography and obscenity and the liberal suspicion of public censorship are not very compatible. Some kind of marriage by compromise is essential if they are going to coexist, but much of the dispute can be patched up if consensus on definitions and meanings of the terms under consideration could be reached. But the sticky side of the issue has its origin in our long proven inability to define "pornography" and "obscenity." It is certain that there are many Christian activists who cannot spell the words but who are positive that they know beyond a shadow of a doubt what is obscene and pornographic and what is not. But nine of the wisest and most respected men in the United States do not know. The ignorance of the latter should be worthy of much more trust than the arrogance of the former; therefore, we shall give considerable weight to their official opinions. A hundred yards can be measured off for a sprint, the weight and price of meat can be marked objectively, and room temperature can be measured the same way in any part of the world. But obscenity lies in a wholly different realm and will continue to resist dogmatic definition.

It is time to make clear that the terms "pornography" and "obscenity" should not be considered synonymous.

The terms have different meanings which the careful critic will observe. Etymologically, the Latin word *obscenus* meant inauspicious, ill-omened, a bad sign. A British authority on the history of pornography, H. Montgomery Hyde, cites Havelock Ellis as suggesting the word may be a corruption of a similar Latin word *scena;* hence, the obscene is anything "off the scene," that is not ordinarily depicted on the stage of life.[1] Today it has come to mean that which is offensive to the taste; something that is foul, abominable, loathsome, disgusting. *Webster's Seventh New Collegiate Dictionary* defines the obscene as "1. disgusting to the senses: repulsive. 2. abhorrent to morality or virtue." The regrettable thing is that in common usage today the word has an exclusively sexual connotation.

"Pornography" is from Greek derivation: *porno* meaning dirty or filthy, and *graphos* meaning writing. Originally it meant a sort of low erotic art, writings of or about prostitutes with the intention of arousing a man's lust so that he would consort with one. In modern usage, the concept of pornography has been enlarged and we will take into account some modern explanations. Suffice it to say, all traditional pornography aims at evoking an erotic response in the individual. In the following discussion of criteria, effects, and possibilities for Christian response, we will be considering "pornography" and "*sexual* obscenity" synonymously. Then we will substantiate the point made by Hyde: "While all pornography is obscene, the converse does not hold good."[2]

---

1. H. Montgomery Hyde, *A History of Pornography* (New York: Farrar, Straus, and Giroux, Inc., 1965), p. 13.
2. *Ibid.*, p. 14.

NOT SEXUAL EXCITEMENT

One concept of pornography deserves discussion because of its widespread acceptance—pornography as sexual material or sexual arousal. Irving Younger states, "Pornography is material that deals with sexual life."[3] Fred Waller, Nashville businessman and co-chairman of a local anti-pornography drive, "We the People Speak, Inc.," defines pornography as "anything either written or in pictures which arouses sexual feelings."[4] The extremism of this definition should be apparent on its face—art soothes and pornography excites—an indefensible dichotomy, as we shall see. Further, the criterion of sexual arousal does nothing to correct the ambiguities of legal definitions of objectionable materials, for what may arouse one viewer may "turn off" most others. There are those aberrants who are excited by the sight of unclothed mannequins in display windows, television ads for bras and girdles, the Sears catalogue, pictures of African natives in *National Geographic*, record album covers, and *Cosmopolitan* cover pictures. It certainly doesn't take pornography to excite excesses of desire among youth; as we all know, there are times when we may be aroused in the complete absence of a physical or external stimulus.

If one accepts this definition, then *The Kiss*, Auguste Rodin's honest expression of love between a man and woman that makes you feel a kind of grandeur for being a human being, is most definitely pornographic. The graceful and tender statute of *The Sleeping Hermaphro-*

---

3. Irving Younger, "Pornography and Violence," *Nation*, August 14, 1967, p. 120.
4. *Nashville Tennessean*, January 11, 1972.

dite would be obscene to many; the *Venus de Milo* might stimulate sexual excitement for tourists, even in her cold station at the Louvre; and Michelangelo's matchless sculpture of the nude David, I suspect, has sent erotic quiver after quiver through many an unmarried school teacher on that summer culture binge in Florence. Voltaire's *Candide* would be pornography and, for that matter, so would several of the plays of Shakespeare which certainly shocked the Cromwellian Puritans.

By this definition, there are some parts of the Bible that could be pornographic to some readers. Read the story of how Lot's two daughters seduced their father into an incestous episode on consecutive nights in Genesis 19:31-36. Or read the poetry of the Song of Solomon that celebrates the joys of sexual love:

> I will sing the song of all songs to Solomon that he may smother me with kisses. Your love is more fragrant than wine. ... Take me with you and we will run together; bring me into your chamber, O King ... He took me into the wine-garden and gave me loving glances. He refreshed me with raisins, he revived me with apricots; for I was faint with love. His left arm was under my head, his right arm was round me.

The bridegroom shares this elation and ecstasy:

> How beautiful are your sandalled feet, O
>   prince's daughter!
> The curves of your thighs are like jewels,
>   the work of a skilled craftsman.
> Your navel is a rounded goblet
>   that never shall want for spiced wine.

Your belly is a heap of wheat
fenced in by lilies.
Your two breasts are like two fawns,
twin fawns of a gazelle.
Your neck is like a tower of ivory.
Your eyes are the pools in Heshbon,
beside the gate of the crowded city.
Your nose is like towering Lebanon
that looks towards Damascus.
You carry your head like Carmel;
the flowing hair on your head is lustrous black,
your tresses are braided with ribbons.
How beautiful, how entrancing you are,
my loved one, daughter of delights!
You are stately as a palm-tree,
and your breasts are the clusters of dates.
I said, 'I will climb up into the palm
to grasp its fronds.'
May I find your breasts like clusters of grapes
on the vine,
the scent of your breath like apricots,
and your whispers like spiced wine
flowing smoothly to welcome my caresses,
gliding down through lips and teeth.[5]

These are just two samples of biblical descriptions of sexual experiences and yet who would claim that their explicitness rendered the passages pornographic?

Further, desire as such is not really a bad thing and there are felicitous times and places when desire should be excited as much as possible and then gratified freely and fully. One critic, Herbert Gold, unequivocally rejects the excitation criterion in determining pornogra-

5. Song of Solomon 1:1-4; 2:4-6; 7:1-9. All Biblical quotations from *The New English Bible* (Oxford University Press, 1970) unless otherwise noted.

phy as opposed to art and notes that "art excites eros, and excites the more the better art is, as a starry night excites, as good news excites."[6] Gold claims that if sexual arousal were the factor identifying pornography that this "would obviously be an argument in favor of pornography . . . In a time of anxiety and boredom we need the love-inciting powers of art more than ever."[7]

THE SUPREME COURT SPEAKS

More than any other institution in the land, the Supreme Court, with its confusing welter of opinions and thousands of words written in celebrated cases, has grappled meaningfully with reality in an attempt to establish relevant criteria clarifying obscenity and pornography. With the benefit of hindsight the whole thing seems like an exercise in futility. In the *Fanny Hill* case (1966), Justice William Brennan, writing for a three-man plurality of the Supreme Court, held that a work is pornographically obscene if it meets three criteria simultaneously:

(1) "The dominant theme of the material taken as a whole must appeal to the prurient interest in sex." To be prurient is to have an itchy, lustful, morbid interest—in this case in the sexual. But what enlightened critic dare declare that another's sexual excitement is lustful rather than wholesome, sick rather than healthy, except in obviously extreme cases? Is it not easy for any of us to rationalize that his sexual curiosity and interests are natural but that the other person's are lustful and depraved?

(2) The material must be "patently offensive because

---

6. Herbert Gold, "The End of Pornography," *Saturday Review*, October 31, 1970, p. 64.
7. *Ibid.*

it affronts contemporary community standards relating to the description or representation of sexual matters." The Court failed to clarify the meaning of "community," but supposing this refers to a county or precinct, what person is capable of assessing "community standards" on such a complex subject?

(3) The material must be "utterly without redeeming social value." In this evolving, complex society of ours, the issue of whether a certain book, play, or movie contains any redeeming social value is one in which no uniformity should be expected from honest and competent philosophers, critics, statesmen, theologians, academics, religious groups, or any other type of group.

As helpful as these three criteria are in guiding individuals in making private decisions, it should be apparent, in the words of dissenting Justice Black, "that human beings, serving either as judges or jurors, could not be expected to give any sort of decision on this element which would even remotely promise any kind of uniformity in the enforcement of this law." Legal determination of obscenity "would depend to a large extent upon the judge's or juror's personality, habits, inclinations, attitudes and other individual characteristics," Black added.[8]

There are some other definitions of pornography that deserve mention because they clarify the concept both in terms of other effects and the intent of the promoter. Two critics of society and the arts have stressed the detachment of pornography from normal emotional contexts.

Novelist-critic J. B. Priestley considers eroticism to be synonymous with pornography and states "it is sexual

---

8. *Ginzburg v. United States*, 383 U.S. 463 (1966).

pleasure without sexual responsibility. Unlike sex, it is not completely natural and it is at the furthest possible remove from love, which is supremely personal."[9] Priestley calls "the encouragement and exploitation of eroticism, sometimes out of hatred of women and fear of real sexual love, but mostly for commercial gain . . . one of the worst features of our Western civilization."[10]

THE ROLE OF CULTURE

Anthropologist Margaret Mead says "we may define pornography, cross-culturally, as words or acts or representations that are calculated to stimulate sex feelings independent of the presence of another loved and chosen human being."[11]

Mead's numerous writings stress the importance of the cultural role in determining what is pornographic and obscene. How often have well-intended citizens and church groups leveled their words and actions against daily behavior, dress style, or artistic efforts that, appraised in an appropriate cultural context, are not obscene or indecent.

Take clothing styles for instance. Before 1966 or 1967, only prostitutes would have appeared on city streets wearing the mini-skirts many young women wear casually today. If the rules on skirt length at the

9. J. B. Priestley, "Eroticism, Sex, and Love," *Saturday Evening Post,* April 27, 1963, p. 10.
10. *Ibid.*
11. From her study "Sex and Censorship in Contemporary Society" in *New World Writing* and quoted in Richard H. Kuh, *Foolish Fig-leaves? Pornography In and Out of Court* (New York: Macmillan Company, 1967), p. 283. The original essay is published as Third Mentor Selection (New York: New American Library, 1953).

church-related college I attended in the early sixties were enforced today by the same standards and with the same zeal and consistency, this college would become virtually an all-male institution overnight. About 1970, a mild controversy was engendered by publicity over the no-bra style. But before the 1920's, the bra was almost unknown in this country. Proper women never wore a brassiere but rather a knit shirt under their slips. The bra first appeared in the "Roaring Twenties" for the purpose of flattening breasts, in accordance with the slim, boyish figure in vogue at that time. The supporting and uplifting bra appeared in the thirties to the horrors of an older generation claiming, "They only wear those things to stick out and attract men." Of course as time passed this garment was accepted by young and old alike as normal and even essential to good taste. One historian of dress fashions suggests that fashion is essentially a game of hide-and-seek, a game depending on prudery and style that has been going on for centuries. Psychologists call it "the theory of the shifting erogenous zone," and it is based on the idea that fashion exploits for a period of time different parts of the female form and when the switch is made by profit-seeking designers the masses consider it "immodest" or "obscene" until it slowly gains acceptance.[12]

---

12. This theory is explained in James Laver, "What Will Fashion Uncover Next?" *Reader's Digest*, September, 1965, pp. 142-45. Laver shows that nearly every recent trend, including toplessness, has its historical antecedents depriving moralists of their claim that the human society has reached "new lows." According to *Women's Wear Daily*, "the newest erogenous zone" will be the hips and posterior. Clothing firms are introducing jean-like pants that feature an inverted U-shaped seam crossing the buttocks. *Newsweek*, September 11, 1972, p. 63.

In reporting how tourists and visitors had defaced and desecrated the new John F. Kennedy Center for Performing Arts, a well-known news magazine lamented that even a young mother sat down on the steps and nursed her baby. One could make a case for this being inappropriate—but obscene or indecent? Hardly! And perhaps in another country, or even among the lower classes in America, this natural act of maternal care would hardly have rated a second glance.

All of what has been said here about culture and pornography substantiates a bald fact: "Custom and acceptance are the great anti-aphrodisiacs. Nothing could be more antiseptic sexually than a nudist colony."[13] Obscenity is largely a relative concept. Few things we label pornographic or sexually obscene are so in and of themselves. Rather, everything must be subjected to the test of appropriateness within a particular context. In what may become the classic definition for its brevity and pungency, Charles Rembar, the Manhattan lawyer who successfully defended *Lady Chatterley's Lover, Tropic of Cancer,* and *Fanny Hill,* offered, "Pornography is in the groin of the beholder."[14]

AESTHETIC DISTANCE AND INTENT

Another of the more useful definitions of pornography is supplied by essayist and novelist George P. Elliott. To Elliott, "pornography is the representation of

---

13. From the report by the Working Party established by a Conference on the Obscenity Laws, under the chairmanship of the Arts Council in Britain.
14. Charles Rembar, *The End of Obscenity* (New York: Bantam Books, 1969), p. 485.

directly or indirectly erotic acts with an intrusive vividness which offends decency without aesthetic justification."[15] Elliott's basic argument is that nothing human should be alien to art—no human feeling or experience should be considered off limits for serious treatment by the artist, not even Judas betraying Jesus, naked hungry Jews crowded by Nazi S. S. soldiers into a gas chamber, nor even husband and wife making love. But the only question is, *how close?* Elliott maintains that, excepting satire, the serious artist establishes a sense of detachment which enables a certain "psychic distance" to be kept between the observer and the observed.[16] Purely for profit the pornographer destroys this aloofness.

We must keep in mind that pornography and erotic realism in the media, difficult as lines of demarcation may be, are not the same thing. Both the technique and the aim of pornography, as well as its purpose for promulgation, are diametrically opposed to artistic realism. If the artist employs erotic realism it is to express a very precious and vital part of man's existence. His primary aim is not profit, though he must eat and live as the rest of us who are benefitted by his efforts. His aim is truth. He does not aim at exciting sexual passion and even though it may come about by coincidence of context, the overall intent is quite different. To the artist, in his efforts to penetrate life and its realities and to communicate their meaning as he has subjectively experienced them, eroticism is woven into the web of

---

15. George P. Elliott, "Against Pornography," *Harper's Magazine,* March, 1965, p. 52.
16. This point is discussed in Stuart W. Little, "Books in Communications—Pornographic Territory," *Saturday Review,* May 10, 1969, p. 81.

his words or images and offered to posterity as a part of life.[17]

Perhaps the best statement on the nature of pornography has been offered by D. H. Lawrence, whose controversial novel *Lady Chatterley's Lover* was not cleared for public distribution in the United States until 1959. Lawrence, often called "the apostle of sex" because he campaigned so vigorously against middle-class prudery, was naturally an enemy of censorship but he also was implacable in his denunciation of pornography. This is evident from his essay "Pornography and Obscenity," published in 1930:

> Even I would censor genuine pornography, rigorously. It would not be very difficult ... Genuine pornography is almost always underworld, it doesn't come into the open ... You can recognize it by the insult it offers, invariably, to sex, and to the human spirit.
>
> Pornography is the attempt to insult sex, to do dirt on it. This is unpardonable. Take the very lowest instance, the picture postcard sold underhand, by the underworld in most cities. What I have seen of them has been of an ugliness to make you cry. The insult to the human body, the insult to a vital human relationship! Ugly and cheap they make the hu-

17. One of the best treatments of this subject is Drs. Eberhard and Phyllis Kronhausen, *Pornography and the Law: The Psychology of Erotic Realism and Pornography* (New York: Ballantine Books, 1959). The volume is based on the premise that the distinction between "hard-core obscenity" and "erotic realism" can be made clear and easily seen and the authors proceed to substantiate this thesis by mustering samples of both kinds of work for comparison. Their analysis involves investigation into content, intent, and structure of the various selections.

man nudity, ugly and degraded they make the sexual act, trivial and cheap and nasty.[18]

The climate of freedom experienced today means that pornography is no longer identifiable as "underworld" but Lawrence's definition of it insulting sex, doing dirt on it, is timeless.

QUESTIONS FOR DISCUSSION

1. Are "pornography" and "obscenity" terms which are highly abstract and in the same category with words like "love," "radical," "liberal," "patriotic," etc.?
2. Why is a definition of pornography as "anything either written or in pictures which arouses sexual feeling" highly inadequate?
3. Can certain passages of the Bible be sexually arousing to certain readers? If so, what stories or writings?
4. Do you think the U.S. Supreme Court is qualified to define obscenity and pornography? If not, what body should assume that burden?
5. What does "a prurient interest in sex" mean?
6. What relevance does a cultural context have in defining obscenity?
7. Should nursing an infant in public be considered obscene in American society?
8. Do you agree that no historical event or human experience should be "off limits" for treatment by the legitimate artist?
9. Are there biblical standards regarding modest dress that are applicable in all cultures (I Timothy 2:9)?
10. How does Paul's sensitivity to the effect of his own actions on other people relate to a Christian's approach to dress (I Corinthians 6:12, 10:23, Romans 14:21)?

---

18. Originally published as *Pornography and Obscenity* by Alfred A. Knopf, Inc., 1930, portions of the above excerpt are reprinted in numerous articles and volumes in the popular literature on this subject. My source is a college reader: William M. Jones, (comp.) *Stages of Composition* (Boston: D. C. Heath and Company, 1964), pp. 151-56, and the selection is chosen as a model of simple and complex definition.

4

Effects of Pornography and Obscenity in Christian Perspective

We have seen that, in moral terms, pornography is an evil. With its use of the media it is the visual and/or literary equivalent to prostitution. But as that great founding father, Benjamin Franklin, once aphorized, sin is not hurtful because it is condemned; rather it is condemned because it is hurtful. And that brings us around to an important question: From the Christian perspective, what are the effects of pornography and sexual obscenity? Should I, as a Christian, consider this issue any differently from the English professor, the law officer, or literary critic? I would like to posit four distinctive effects the Christian should consider with special gravity.

INTRUDES UPON PRIVACY AND INDIVIDUALITY

First, the Christian should have no truck with pornography because it offends the right of privacy and man's sense of individuality. It intrudes upon the rights of others. Respect for the individual as a unique person, respect for his rights, his judgments, his feelings, his dignity as a human, is more than just the foundation of democracy—this concept is at the very core of Christian faith. Woven into the whole theme of biblical theology is the concept that man is different, his soul is priceless, his rights are inviolable. Man was created as an animal with a difference. He has a unique sense of individual privacy with a concomitant capacity for shame or embarrassment when this privacy is violated. Man almost instinctively has habits of behavior or dress to make certain his "private parts" are indeed private; this may vary from culture to culture, but in practically all primitive tribes male and female alike cover their private parts and do not copulate before public gaze. Besides all kinds of sex relations, this sense of privacy is usually extended to other individual bodily functions such as eating, bathing, defecating, and urinating and to special forms of behavior and circumstances like weeping and human suffering.

As fellow humans we respect the individuality and privacy of others. Eating may not seem like such a private function since it is often done in public, but have you ever felt uneasy because you were at the table with friends and the only one eating? You know what the response would be if you were to stop eating and fix your eyes in a stare at someone across the counter or at the next table. One way a movie director can produce absurdity is by showing his principals masticating food zoomed in at the closest possible range.

Suppose a television documentary on various hospital patients were to show at close range the physical suffering of a terminal patient who had lost consciousness, or zoomed in on a mother as her child begins to make its appearance in the world, or on a man so overcome with excrutiating pain that we see filmed evidence he had lost all control over his bladder and bowels, or of a nauseated person vomiting up his food unexpectedly. Such a documentary would give us feelings of great discomfort because we would have been invited by the media to obscenely invade the privacy of other individuals.

In watching the evening news, there's something discomfiting about miners' wives as they turn grief-stricken upon seeing the lifeless bodies of their husbands removed from mother earth. We look down or turn away to avoid observing the grief of survivors at a funeral or graveyard ceremony. Separate toilet or shower stalls in public facilities give the user psychological security. A gynecologist puts up a sheet for the same reason and wears rubber gloves for more than health regulations. And we know that modern criminal ethics reassured the victim of the electric chair that the hideous sight of his execution would not be exposed to the leering public. (Had this sight *been* given to the public one might suppose that the Supreme Court would have ruled capital punishment a "cruel and unjust punishment" long before 1972!)

In sum, obscenity consists in making the private public, in exposing to public view intimate and personal experiences of life for the sole purpose of arousing lust, inducing shock, or exploiting morbid interest. And in no area is this privacy violated so much as in sexuality. We have already noted that very few motion pictures, outside of Disney Productions and other G-rated films, are void of some kind of bed scene or nudity involving the main characters. Since this is as true of good films as of the bad, it means literally that we cannot sit through a serious movie these days without becoming a thirdhand party to somebody else's simulated sex. With or without our approval, we become involuntary voyeurs of the synthetic intimacy of others. A more recent innovation than simulated intercourse, obviously aimed more at evoking humor by mild shock than showing us that the characters are human, is showing the male leads in urination or at the stool. Not that these scenes are reprehensible but they are so personal, so dull, that serious intrusion is displeasing and any other intrusion is exploitative.

Since a healthy sexuality is such a vital part of a normal human existence, Christians must have concern for its protection against the forces which tend to distort or weaken it. This whole issue of pornography as an intrusion upon individual privacy has perhaps been raised most forcibly in the writings of the distinguished writer and critic, George Steiner. He questions the liberal assumption, also shared by many Christians, that the torrents of pornography are any longer worth defending in the name of freedom. He comments that "future historians may come to characterise the present era in the West as one of a massive onslaught on human privacy, on the delicate processes by which we seek to become our own singular selves, to hear the echo of our specific being."[1]

More specifically, Steiner questions a policy of "total statement" because we have lived through too much actual sadism in our time to justify much energy defending and encouraging its explicit literary description. Writers who are obsessed with detailed clinical descriptions of sex could profit by studying the thrilling and engaging but skillful and indirect way it was treated by Eliot or Tolstoy. "Sexual relations are, or should be, one of the citadels of privacy;" sexuality should be guarded as "the nightplace where we must be allowed to gather the splintered and harried elements of our con-

1. George Steiner, "Night Words: High Pornography and Human Privacy," *Encounter*, 25 (October, 1965), 17.

sciousness to some kind of inviolate order and repose. It is in sexual experience that a human being alone, and two human beings in that attempt at total communication which is also communion, can discover the unique bent of their identity . . . The new pornographers subvert this last, vital privacy. They take away the words of the night and shout them over the roof-tops, making them hollow."[2]

Steiner concludes that the worst present danger to our inward freedom and the freedom of literature is neither censorship nor verbal reticence. "The danger," he claims, "lies in the facile contempt which the erotic novelist exhibits for his readers, for his personages, and for the language. Our dreams are marketed wholesale."[3]

If Steiner's claim has validity, and common sense affirms that it does, and if we value individuality and the right to privacy—especially in an age when our burgeoning population and the electronic inroads into our daily lives make real privacy less attainable—then we as Christians must deplore the way in which the most intimate aspects of human life are denigrated by over-publicity.

ANTITHESIS OF CHRISTIAN ATTITUDES

Second, the Christian must stand opposed to pornography because it is diametrically opposed to and at war against the kind of Christ-like attitudes we are expected to possess.

---

2. *Ibid.*
3. *Ibid.* p. 19. See another discussion of this point in Harvey G. Cox, "Sexuality and Responsibility: A New Phase," in *Sexual Ethics and Christian Responsibility*, ed. John Charles Wynn (New York: Association Press, 1970), pp. 25-36.

No right-thinking Christian would argue against as full and healthy a sex life as each person is capable of living. And we must be honest and admit that if any one institution has been more to blame for promoting prudery, restricting honest sexual communication, inhibiting sex education, promoting the double standard, and blocking healthy attitudes, it has been the Christian church. "The traditional view of Christian civilizations has been that all forms of sexual activity are by nature suspect," states Alex Comfort, "and that only those that mke up a bare minimum necessary for the purposes of reproduction, are permissible."[4]

So our history has been pretty sorry. And as we move toward the twenty-first century, where less physical energy need be expended in earning a living, and where the work week is slowly being reduced to thirty and then maybe to twenty hours, it is all the more important that the church reaffirm and promote the creative role of sexuality toward insuring a normal, happy life in adjustment to "future shock."

But acknowledging and correcting the mistakes of the past should not lead us to bend too far in the other direction and offer uncritical endorsement and even celebration of every book, film, play, or magazine produced under the banner of the so-called new freedom. Such a response would lead, quite possibly, to a personal view of sexuality that is equally as detrimental and unhealthy. Let us note why this is true.

Objectionable erotic materials may produce an attitude of compartmentalizing sex into a totally separate aspect of life, making sex a purely physical exercise.

4. Author of *Sex and Society* and quoted in *Commonweal* January 12, 1968, p. 438.

With this attitude people find sex to be more *repression* than *expression;* they become unfulfilled, empty, and discontented. This is not referring to men who, traveling alone, find themselves tempted to flip through the pages of a "girlie" magazine at the airport or bus newsstand. It refers to those who are obsessed with eroticism, who feel that they need it regularly to make life enriching. Actually they are acting as though they were living in a society of adolescents. You may remember when you were a teen-ager and just beginning to have the feelings and curiosities that accompany puberty, but you were a little callow and uncertain of those feelings and emotions. Because it was fun, sexual activities were engaged in for the sake of sex. As you grew older you learned that sexual expression was more enjoyable with ·the person whom you actually liked. And then as you got older you were able to validate the point you heard forwarded by parents, preachers, and advisers—that sex is much more rewarding and much more enjoyable, fun if you will, with the person you love and to whom you have committed your life.

Now pornography distorts this basic healthy approach to sex. It promotes an attitude that views sex as a consummatory, even meaningless,[5] and certainly masturbatory activity. A person is all alone with sex just as when he was an adolescent. You don't have relations with a person; you only seem to.

------

5. "Consummatory" and "instrumental" are terms taken from communication theory. Persuasive communication always aims at changing behavior in the future and is thus "instrumental." "Consummatory" communication is to be enjoyed for the moment (e.g., a joke) and to be forgotten. Consummatory sex aims at nothing more than the pleasure of the moment; any future consideration or effect is not to be taken into account.

Not only does pornography foster an unhealthy attitude toward sex but it promotes an un-Christ-like attitude toward other people. The New Testament makes clear that the Christian life is a radically new life. "Adapt yourselves no longer to the pattern of this present world," enjoined the apostle Paul, "but let your minds be remade and your whole nature thus transformed. Then you will be able to discern the will of God, and to know what is good, acceptable, and perfect."[6] Few demands of the new life in Christ are made clearer than God's expectation that we keep our minds and bodies from the impurities of fornication[7] and lust. St. Paul exhorted the young minister Timothy to "Flee youthful lusts."[8] In writing to the Corinthian Christians, he said:

> Do you not know that your bodies are limbs and organs of Christ? Shall I then take from Christ his bodily parts and make them over to a harlot? Never! You surely know that anyone who links himself with a harlot becomes physically one with her. . . . Do you not know that your body is a shrine of the indwelling Holy Spirit, and the Spirit is God's gift to you? You do not belong to yourselves; you were bought at a price. Then honour God in your body.[9]

Perhaps more appropriate for this topic is Paul's statement to the Ephesians:

---

6. Romans 12:2.
7. Incidentally, both *fornication* and *pornography* come from the same Greek word.
8. II Timothy 2:22, KJV.
9. I Corinthians 6:15-20.

In a word, as God's dear children, try to be like him, and live in love as Christ loved you, and gave himself up on your behalf as an offering and sacrifice whose fragrance is pleasing to God. Fornication and indecency of any kind, or ruthless greed, must not be so much as mentioned among you, as befits the people of God. No coarse, stupid, or flippant talk; these things are out of place; you should rather be thanking God. For be very sure of this: no one given to fornication or indecency, or the greed which makes an idol of gain, has any share in the kingdom of Christ and of God.

Let no one deceive you with shallow arguments; it is for all these things that God's dreadful judgment is coming upon his rebel subjects. Have no part or lot with them. For though you were once all darkness, now as Christians you are light. Live like men who are at home in daylight, for where light is, there all goodness springs up, all justice and truth.[10]

To the Colossians he admonished, "Let your thoughts dwell on that higher realm. . . . Then put to death those parts of you which belong to the earth—fornication, indecency, lust, foul cravings, and the ruthless greed which is nothing less than idolatry."[11]

A popular position, of course, is that no normal person is seriously changed by pornography or sexual obscenity. "No girl has ever been seduced by a book," is an oft-repeated generalization undergirding such logic. To claim that objectionable materials do not lead their

10. Ephesians 5:1-9.
11. Colossians 3:1, 5.

users to criminal or antisocial behavior is to say one thing (and we shall examine that claim later). But to say that the purveyance and regular ingestion of pornography does not so alter a person's attitude and perception of humanity in such a way so as to be displeasing to his Creator is to claim something else!

Taken literally, the above statement is true. Books in the physical sense do not do anything, including seducing girls. Books do, however, instill in their serious readers ideas and attitudes that later give birth to action, either good or ill. The comment of poet-librarian Felix Pollak on this point is apropos. "The saying doesn't do the cause of literature any good, or the intellectual cause in general. If one denies the power of the word to do evil," he claims, "one denies the power of the word to do good. In effect, one denies the power of the word. I prefer the healthy fear and awe of the written and spoken word, evidence by censorious zealots, to the wishy-washy neutralism of the liberalist anti-censors."[12]

If a man's attitudes are affected by his environment, by his reading, by his public and religious education, by the happenings in his life, he must then be affected by a steady exposure to pornography in the media. The effects on his attitudes and frame of reference cannot be neutral. Simple elimination will mean that if pornography is incapable of effecting a betterment of attitudes, the practical result will be detrimental to our spiritual welfare. The point made by some ministers that poring over pornography is the equivalent of lustful, illicit desire may be suspect for overgeneralization. But we cannot afford to take lightly the teaching of Jesus on the Mount: "You have learned that they were told, 'Do not commit adultery.' But what I tell you is this: If a

---

12. Quoted in *Time*, April 5, 1971, p. 64.

man looks on a woman with a lustful eye, he has already committed adultery with her in his heart."[13]

Of course the main reason this whole matter of what pornography does to our attitudes and beliefs is so important to the Christian is that our beliefs and attitudes give birth to actions. The two are linked inseparably and unavoidably. Through their observations and scientific investigations, psychologists have long substantiated what Solomon stated so succinctly over twenty centuries ago: "For as he thinketh in his heart, so is he."[14]

No brazen claim is made here that anyone who reads pornography will rush out and commit fornication or adultery with the first willing partner. It does seem logical, however, that one's moral stamina could be weakened by a surfeit of self-indulgence, that one's will to remain pure is reduced. No doubt different people react in different ways. But one thing is certain. Pornography offers no deliberate encouragement to moral purity or steadfastness. Read again the list of Christian virtues listed in the Epistle to the Galatians: love, joy, peace, patience, kindness, goodness, fidelity, gentleness, and self-control. Which of these virtues can be promoted by the pornographer? Christians are admonished: "Whatever you are doing, whether you speak or act, do everything in the name of the Lord Jesus, giving thanks to God the Father through him."[15] Can a Christian devour pornography to the glory of Christ? We are admonished: "Let this mind be in you, which was also in Christ Jesus."[16] If excessive exposure to erotic films

---

13. Matthew 5:27-28
14. Proverbs 23:7, KJV.
15. Colossians 3:17.
16. Phillippians 2:5, KJV; the Phillips translation reads: "Let Christ Jesus be your example as to what your attitude should be."

and literature causes a man to mentally undress every attractive woman he sees, as one not so young fellow once admitted, could he possibly have the mind of Christ?

Out of the realm of opinion and attitude change, but worth consideration is this question: If the Christian takes seriously the responsibilities of stewardship of his time and money, can pornography be justified even at best as a harmless diversion?

As an aside, we can see that pornography distorts proper Christian attitudes by the extent of rationalizing and circumlocution among pornographers. One thing that leads to frustration in all people is having to reconcile two opposing beliefs or convictions that we hold to be valid. A man who sees inconsistencies in his beliefs will strive to change these conditions and thus return to an original and preferred state of consistency.[17] Har-

---

17. The theory of consistency and its relation to behavior is the product of several writers who have used different terms to describe concepts that are largely similar. Leon Festinger *A Theory of Cognitive Dissonance;* (Evanston, Ill.: Row, Peterson & Co, 1957) uses the terms "consonance" (consistency) and "dissonance" (inconsistency) to describe the relationship between two elements of belief. Charles E. Osgood and Percy H. Tannenbaum ("The Principle of Congruity in the Prediction of Attitude Change," *Psychological Review,* Vol. 62, 1955, pp. 42-55) use the terms "congruity" and "incongruity" to discuss the relationships among three elements of belief; these elements include an individual's attitude toward some topic (person, place, thing, concept, subject matter, etc.), his attitude toward a second person who expresses an attitude toward the topic, and the attitude that that second person expresses. These three elements may fit "congruently" or "incongruently." Fritz Heider *(The Psychology of Interpersonal Relations;* New York: John Wiley & Sons, Inc., 1958) uses the terms "balance" (consistency) and "imbalance" (inconsistency) to describe similar sets of three beliefs. Another writer, Theodore Newcomb ("An Approach to the Study of Communicative Acts," *Psychological Review,* Vol. 60, 1953, pp. 393-404), speaks of "symmetry" (consistency) and "asymmetry" (inconsistency) of beliefs.

monizing conflicting beliefs leads to rationalization, a mental process in which justification is based on desire. How would, for example, a young woman harmonize a belief in at least a modicum of decent dress with her desire to earn the money she could make as a nude dancer or stripteaser? In the words of one dancer, stripping should not be viewed "as being any different from anybody else's job." To her, the work was just as noble as secretarial work except for the hours of work. "The only real difference I can see is that the secretary uses her fingers (for typing, etc.) and I have to use everything I've got to make a living.[18] One of the most absurd rationalizations that is frequently heard among the nudity in media advocates is that being in the altogether is somehow more honest, more innocent, more peaceful, even more spiritual than being dressed.[19] One actress of several erotic and/or nude plays, Sally Kirkland, argued that "There is nothing more innocent and vulnerable than the naked human body. When we come to the day and the year when no one in this country feels funny about taking off his clothes, then we've come to a very healthy time. . . . With nudity, we'll get some honesty, which we haven't had in the arts in a long time."[20]

---

18. *Nashville Tennessean*, July 17, 1972.
19. This point has long been argued by advocates of social nudism who have tried to idealize the human condition. It is true, as Leonard Blank points out, that "sex, class and power are less relevant in a nude society and suspension of these artificial barriers increases togetherness." Blank adds, however, that "even in the nudist camp there are personality clashes, cliques, and intergroup disagreements. Not everyone finds a utopia there." New status symbols emerge when old ones are impossible; for example, the "cottontail" is a negative status symbol. See "Nudity," *Psychology Today*, June, 1969, pp. 18-23.
20. *Time*, July 11, 1969, pp. 64-65.

Rudi Gernreich, designer of the scandalous topless bathing suit in 1964, has argued that his see-through and braless styles give women of our time "greater and greater freedom."[21] Actress Shelley Winters, approaching fifty, parodied the "clotheslessness-is-next-to-Godliness" line in a statement about media nudity: "I think it is disgusting, shameful and damaging to all things American. But if I were twenty-two with a great body, it would be artistic, tasteful, patriotic and a progressive, religious experience."[22]

Our language choices are certainly a revealer of our beliefs and attitudes. Not only that, but our language helps to mold the world we see. When words like lustful, lewd, indecent, and promiscuous are replaced by words like fantasy, sophisticated, exotic dancing, and swinging, there may be, at least from the Christian perspective, a serious attitudinal problem.

I want to avoid presumptuous preaching in the study. But for the Spirit-led child of God, the issue is clear:

If you are guided by the Spirit you will not fulfil the desires of your lower nature. That nature sets its desires against the Spirit, while the Spirit fights against it. They are in conflict with one another so that what you will to do you cannot do. But if you are led by the Spirit, you are not under law.

Anyone can see the kind of behaviour that belongs to the lower nature: fornication, impurity, and indecency; idolatry and sorcery; quarrels, a contentious temper, envy, fits of

21. *Newsweek*, April 14, 1969, p. 70.
22. *Time*, July 11, 1969, p. 63.

rage, selfish ambitions, dissensions, party in-
trigues, and jealousies; drinking bouts, orgies,
and the like. I warn you, as I warned you
before, that those who behave in such ways
will never inherit the kingdom of God.[23]

DEGRADES AND DISHONORS HUMAN DIGNITY

Christians know that the ethic of Jesus, indeed the
ethics of the entire New Testament, demands that we be
in right relationship with our fellowman. We cannot be
in right relationship to our Father, for that matter we
cannot love him,[24] unless we are in right relationship
with our fellowman. Christian ethics is essentially *social*
ethics. With this in mind, we look at a third reason a
Christian stands opposed to pornography and obscenity—it degrades and exploits other human beings made
in the image of God. Pornography poisons our minds
against other persons, degrades and dishonors the
uniquely human dimensions of life, and eventually cuts
off lines of genuine communication.

Throughout the Bible, beginning with the story of
creation in Genesis, we see that man is different from
the other elements of creation. As a creature who is
more than an animal and who is made in the very image
of God, man was endowed with a conscience, a moral
law, and the ability to discern good from evil. Then man
was and continues to be challenged to discipline himself
in the face of his unprecedented freedom. His dual
purpose is to think and act in such a way that will bring
glory to his Creator and be a blessing to other men. In a

---

23. Galatians 5:16-21.
24. I John 4:20.

general sense he is a brother to the remainder of human creation. He is called to love his fellowman and use wisely the material blessings under his stewardship. The pornography consumer distorts this life style by "using" people to serve selfish purposes. To such a person, other people must be exploited. They are stripped of personality and exist only as a "sex animal" or some kind of "sex machine." To quote Susan Sontag: "What pornographic literature does is precisely to drive a wedge between one's existence as a sexual being—while in ordinary life a healthy person is one who prevents such a gap from opening up."[25] This comment on the effect of pornography comes from a fair and able critic who writes in *defense* of pornography.

How are people exploited by pornography? Well, the trappings have been different from age to age, but all pornography is about alike. Sexually obscene materials "operate within highly conventionalized formulas of low-grade sadism, excremental drollery, and banal fantasies of phallic prowess or feminine responsiveness," writes Steiner. "In its own way the stuff is as predictable as a Boy Scout manual."[26]

As for the pornographic photographer, artist, or film producer, the focus is zoomed in for intense concentration on the genitals and accessory sex organs. He is so preoccupied with these disembodied (pardon!) body-possessing organs that they are emphasized to the point of distortion. The pornographer is concerned with ways these sex organs can be used to titillate, stimulate, or be stimulated. These sex organs are devoid of any other

25. *New York Times Magazine*, March 28, 1971, p. 24. See her book *Styles of Radical Will.*
26. "Night Words," p. 15.

meaning—the other parts of the body, the personality, the mind and feelings have no place. The worth of the "person" can be measured in no other way than the length of the penis or size of the breasts or some other such measurement, whatever the case may be. Such views as are rarely seen by a near-sighted gynecologist are by their very nature created for the voyeur, or for supplying masturbatory fantasies to those who may feel deprived of, or dissatisfied by, normal and healthy stimulation.

The pornographic writer, of course, is concerned with the same effect but he must go about it without the benefit of visual aids. If he is going to produce a book that competes favorably on the porno market, adding a flare or two of "redeeming value" is not nearly so important as constantly keeping before the reader's mind a succession of erotically stimulating images. The best way to begin the story is with a mildly erotic scene, but not to throw out the most sensual scenes until near the end. That way the writer can progress from events that are "hot" to "hotter" to "hottest" and the reader will not be disappointed. But the writer must unfold his story rapidly. He must not bore the reader with material that tells us his characters are real persons with real ideas and emotions and a sense of noble purpose in life. Such nonerotic development is superfluous and will only be scanned to "get to the good stuff." The idea is to keep the reader's mind focused on erotic word-images and not to distract him with the side issues of scenery, character, and personality portrayal.[27]

The effect of all this has already been made clear.

---

27. See Kronhausens, "The Psychology of Pornography" in *Pornography and the Law*, pp. 175-244.

Pornography depersonalizes sex and exalts it for its own sake. It represents and feeds upon compulsive sexual occupation. A person is not looked upon for the love and compassion that can be communicated in a meaningful relationship. In fact, the role of emotion must be completely divorced from the experience of the moment—it is sexual *activity* as opposed to *feeling* that is exalted. Love is reduced to an interplay of sex organs. The persons portrayed are not outlined as real persons; they are merely the suppliers of sex organs and activity. Pornography preaches two propagandist messages: (1) that love is not essential to sex, that love is an invention and has a limited congruence with sex; and, (2) that sexual experience exists for its own sake, a kind of genitalia á go-go in which cerebral or true emotional communion can only dull its sensation. If the viewer or reader is unable to achieve sexual gratification pornography leaves him unsatisfied and frustrated.

In this connection it is worth noting that this turning of sex into an obscenity is not a mutual and equal transaction, but is rather an act of exploitation and prostitution perpetrated by males upon women. Woman is degraded as in no other manner. Pornography is generally produced by men for men.[28] This may be because a woman's sexual response is ordinarily more suffused with human emotion than is man's and men are more easily satisfied with autoerotic activities. Whatever

28. This may be rapidly changing. There are some writers and publishers who are aiming at the female audience. See *Newsweek*, December 27, 1971, p. 63. The latest fad is the production of nude male pin-up type calendars for women. *Newsweek*, September 11, 1972, p. 56. Heretofore, the most famous example of a female pornographer is the anonymous authoress of "The Story of O" but even it was written with a male audience in mind. The U. S. Commission discovered that women are virtually as interested in erotica as men.

the explanation, women's "libbers" are agreed that pornography is a "sexist" tool used against them to deprive
them of their dignity.

This exploitation of women's humanity is evident in
any kind of pornography. In some of the hard-core
books and magazines women are treated as canisters of
human flesh to be chained and raped, lashed with whips,
trampled upon, or have their nipples seared with ciga-
rettes. The injustice must be evident. If such descriptions were written about "castrating and torturing
blacks," comments columnist Pete Hamill, "there would
be court orders everywhere."[29]

But pornography in the printed media is no worse an
exercise in humiliation than performed pornography
such as in sex shows and nude dancing. When there are
men involved they are not exactly being ennobled but
neither quite so exploited. They are viewed as masters,
men upon whom mother nature and good luck have
smiled so that they are appointed vicars for the entire
male audience. As Stanley Kauffman points out:

> Performed porno is a species of male re-
> venge on our social systems of courtship and
> monogamy, courtship in which a man has to
> woo a woman to get her to bed or wed him or
> both, monogamy in which he has nominally
> to forego the favors of other women all his
> life in order to get hers. Performed porno
> makes every man a sultan.[30]

What a contrast all of this is from the life and teach-

---

29. From his column in *New York Post*, July 13, 1970 and
quoted in Maisie Ward, "Speaking of Sex . . . and so forth,"
America, June 12, 1971, p. 614.
30. Stanley Kauffman, "On Obscenity," *The New Republic*, October 17, 1970, p. 35.

ings of Christ. If any lesson should be learned by his identification with the Samaritan woman at the well, the woman caught in adultery, the unscrupulous tax collector Zaccheus, and the downtrodden and lonely, it is that people—their happiness, their feelings, their attitudes, and, most important, their eternal souls—are the most valuable, the most important part of God's creation. Any act that deprives them of a noble existence, disregards their feelings, distorts their values, and destroys their souls—such an act is sinfully obscene.

DELETERIOUS EFFECT ON SOCIETY

The final reason the Christian must be opposed to pornography and obscenity is because of the potential deleterious effect upon group units within a society. Here our interest is extended beyond the realm of the individual to the familial and other institutional units and to society as a whole. "For no one of us lives, and equally no one of us dies, for himself alone."[31] If the masses within a society are indifferent to pornography, what effect will this have on home life? on our schools? on our churches? on our society as a whole? The fact that this question has been frequently answered by religious folk in the most authoritarian and dogmatic manner must not obscure its importance.

Among the most libertarian of us, few would grant that pornography and obscenity are harmless. To argue that artistic endeavor can lift up a society and give it renewed spirit and taste and then to deny that any prostitution of artistic expression has cultural consequences must be the height of inconsistency. John P.

---

31. Romans 14:7.

Newport points out the irony of television or movie executives who argue that sex and violence in the movies and on television has little harmful influence and with their advertising clients seek to demonstrate their media can have tremendous influence in selling consumer goods.[32] The only question is the nature and extent of the effect.

Regrettably, the effects of objectionable materials cannot be quantified in an experimental psychology laboratory. "One cannot simulate in the laboratory the existence or nonexistence of a lifelong exposure to or preoccupation with obscenity," states Harvard Government Professor James Q. Wilson, "any more than one can simulate a lifelong exposure to racist or radical opinions."[33] Since quantitative evidence cannot be mustered we must argue from analogy or seek the insight of philosophers, theologians, and historians.

A favorite analogy of preachers is to compare America with the Roman empire. But the factors that cause a great empire to rise and later weaken and fall are so many, so complex, and so interwoven with the exigencies of time and place that the pulpit has undoubtedly been guilty of gross oversimplification. In fact, many of our ideas and images about the old Roman empire may be based more on the cinemepics of Cecil B. DeMille than on reliable history. The celebrated immorality of emperors such as Nero and Caligula had occurred hundreds of years before and may have had little to do with the empire's fall. Historians note that the empire actually began to collapse subsequent to its conversion to

32. John P. Newport, "Sexuality in the Contemporary Arts," *Review and Expositor,* 68 (Spring, 1971), 214.
33. From an essay in *The Public Interest* and quoted in *Time,* April 5, 1971, p. 64.

"Christianity" in 313 A. D., when the family of Constantine split it into three parts and each began a conspiracy against the other two. In 325 A.D. persecution of non-Christian sects began. And as Gibbon points out in his classic work that has been quoted many a time in American pulpits, non-Christians—together with all Christians who disagreed with the theologians closest to the emperor—were subject to torture, arrest, and even death. Thus, when Rome fell to the barbarians in the fifth century, it had been officially "Christian" for 120 years.

Come across the centuries and look at the Scandinavian countries where the freedom and openness has made them internationally notorious. What is the quality of their society?[34] For practical purposes, the role and influence of organized religion has all but disappeared from the scene. Regular worship attendance is unknown to the masses. The Bible is not taken authoritatively. Premarital sex is taken for granted by the vast majority of young people. Today America seems to be rapidly moving in that direction. Is this the kind of society most Americans want? Before answering that question, I suggest we consider the possibility there are more ways to measure the decency and humaneness of a society than by such factors as virginity rate and pornography laws or lack of same. It just could be that the quality of education, health and medical care, the mental health of citizens, the rate of violent crime, the place granted the aging, the relationship with other nations, and the way its citizens resolve their differences might also have bearing on relevant criteria.

---

34. For one journalistic look at the Scandinavian countries, see "The Contraceptive Society," *Look*, February 4, 1969, pp. 50ff.

Many observers are quite concerned about the sadistic component of much contemporary pornography. "For some, reading a pornographic book may satisfy their sadistic impulses vicariously," notes psychoanalyst Ernest Van den Haag, and for others "there will be a temptation to emulate the sadism communicated in the book or magazine or movie or play."[35] Dr. Van den Haag believes the cumulative effect of sadism "contributes to a general atmosphere where sadism becomes permissible as far as a large mass of people are concerned."[36] In evidence of this, he cites the example of *Der Sturmer*, a Hitlerite journal that mixed anti-Semitism and sex which contributed to the general atmosphere of apathy that made it possible to slaughter Jews with little protest. "Natural selection tells of limbs and functions that atrophy through lack of use," warns George Steiner, adding that "the power to feel, to experience and realize the precarious uniqueness of each other's being, can also wither in a society."[37]

From the Christian perspective, parents must be concerned about any potential noxious effect of pornographic materials on the moral fiber of the family. If we should concede that pornography and obscenity have absolutely no ill effects on the thinking and action of normal, mature adults, then what about the effect on children? Anyone knows that pornography stashed away in hiding may eventually trickle down to the children and then be shared surreptitiously with the neighbor's children. You probably remember from your

35. In interview, "What's Happening to American Morals?" *U. S. News and World Report*, January 25, 1971, p. 72.
36. *Ibid.*
37. "Night Words," p. 18.

own childhood and adolescence that the quarantining of offspring develops some leaks.

But quarantining failures are hardly the most serious ones. Young people feel that they are instilled with more sophistication, dignity, and freedom by emulating the "advanced" tastes of their forebears. If a parent tells the child of the value of studying the Bible and reading good books but he or she is always found with a tawdry pornographic or semipornographic novel, what do you think will be the effect? If the father gets his jollies at a topless bar, or leaves the kids with momma to ride the roller coaster while he slips into the strip show at the state fair, it may seem disingenuous to attempt to convince his sons that sex is actually a God-given means of expressing and enhancing love, and his daughters may disregard the preacher's lesson that teaches female modesty is more desirable than crass exhibitionism. If our children see that the most hilarious lines of a movie or television show are those that embody a dirty joke, obscene or profane language, it will be pretty difficult to convince them that filthy speech and chronic reliance on shocking listeners by profanity mirrors a disrespect for the name of God and the inability to use effectively the ordinary powers of speech. The many maxims about children ignoring our words and following our example ("I'd rather see a sermon than hear one any day," and that kind of thing) could be evoked with profit at this point.

This point is not going to be pushed too far. Hopefully I have presented enough reason and opinion to substantiate a serious concern for a potential pernicious effect that excessive obscenity can have on larger interpersonal groups in society. Detailed considerations of possible antisocial or criminal behavior were not intended with this point; we will touch on that later. From the Christian perspective, pornography or sexual obscenity is a moral and spiritual issue, and a Christian response should rest as much upon ethical and philosophical, as utilitarian considerations. What, then, should be the Christian response? We turn next to a consideration of formal, public censorship.

QUESTIONS FOR DISCUSSION

1. Can you think of personal instances in which there was mild discomfort because you felt you were invading another's privacy?
2. Do you agree with the author that analogies comparing the U. S. with ancient Rome are sometimes farfetched?
3. What are the qualities of a nation that make it a decent, moral, and humane society of people?
4. Do you believe there is less privacy in America now than ever before?
5. Do you agree that the church has been one of the major institutions which over the centuries has inhibited healthy sexual communication and attitudes? If so, why do you think this has been true?
6. The New Testament warns many times against the sin of lust. How should a Christian define lust?
7. How should a Christian refute the argument "No girl has ever been seduced by a book"?
8. Can pornography be justified as a harmless diversion?
9. Christians have long been admonished to "love people and use things" and not vice versa. How does a pornography consumer violate this principle?
10. Why is true love more than interplay of sex organs?
11. Do you agree that pornography has traditionally degraded and humiliated women more than men?
12. Do you agree that there is little adults can hide from their children?

5

Considering Censorship

Censorship is a dirty word—one of the very dirtiest. It is one of those vexing issues upon which we should never expect unanimity. If you are to follow the lines of reasoning pursued in the rest of this study (much less concur), we will need to define our terms. It is particularly important that we distinguish between "censorship" and "control." Censorship constitutes the legal imposition of restraints upon the production, publication, and sales of some photograph, film, art object, book, magazine, or other reading material in order to make it unavailable to the general public as well as upon the production or performance of any public entertainment.[1] If a play were legally halted in order to insure the physical protection of the safety of an audience, say in the case of a fire hazard, this would *not* be censorship. Control is practiced by those who have no legal authority to censor or threaten to censor but use persuasion and even coercion to restrict freedom of speech; it follows that they have no legal power to prosecute those deemed offenders. Put simply, the objectives of censor-

---

1. See this definition of terms in Robert W. Haney, *Comstockery in America—Patterns of Censorship and Control* (Boston: Beacon Press, 1960) pp. 6-7.

ship and control are identical but the means are different.

The concept of censorship is, of course, an old one and rather sophisticated in its application. Historically, it has applied almost exclusively to those few cultures where literacy has developed. Going back to biblical times, man's original fear seems to have been directed largely toward communication that was deemed blasphemous. As the power of the political state developed, public concern over blasphemy seems to have abated and the fear of seditious and treasonous utterances arose as a peril to the sovereignty of the Crown. Now with most of the world literate and reasonably intelligent so that they can elect and exercise some control over their leaders, the crime of sedition has been greatly reduced. The practical result is that when one thinks of censorship, he is thinking of this concept as applied to obscenity (with the possible and important exception of the government's control over the flow of information to its citizens).

The interesting thing is that there are so very few people who feel they could be corrupted by any concept or depiction—whether blasphemous, seditious, or obscene. Perhaps an admission of vulnerability may make a person seem weak or close-minded. In our times, sophisticated people seem to take pride in refusing to be shocked. The censorious are worried only about the souls of others rather than themselves. The practical result of this generalization is that, since Freud, the public image of the censor has been that of an insecure person with a twisted mind who, afraid others may be enjoying themselves more than they should, is bent on imposing his emotional hangups upon his less inhibited fellows. Censorship is unfortunately equated with dictatorships, temporal and spiritual. It is big brotherism and 1984.

This will not be a detailed analysis of the pros and cons of censorship. The published literature on this issue is abundant and if the reader wants to pursue the matter beyond the synthesis and interpretation here the documentation and bibliography may be consulted with profit.

Censorship is one of those exasperatingly complicated and elusive subjects that perplex the mind so much that those who grapple with it are tempted to plunge toward one extreme or the other. And history has shown that the *easiest* thing to censor, if not the most important, is something of a sexual nature. Some minister, priest, judge, or well-known citizen merely has to tell the media he is morally offended and in breathless, Bible-tapping guilt, a large part of the community is likely to rise up and offer united support for suppression.

While numerous state and local communities have their own pornography and obscenity statutes, sometimes enforced and often neglected, total freedom and permissiveness within certain realms of entertainment media have been established in most parts of the country. The Roth case before the Supreme Court in 1957 held obscenity statutes, in general, to be constitutional. But succeeding interpretations have knocked them down. Literary censorship has been virtually abolished. In a 1969 decision, *Stanley v. Georgia*, the Court ruled that obscenity, when it is read or viewed at home, is protected by the Constitution. This decision implies, to many constitutional lawyers, the right to buy or receive obscenity. Decision after decision has opened wider the umbrella of the First Amendment.

Can Christians take comfort in the law of the land as

it has evolved? Or should we concur with those among us who stigmatize the Supreme Court as the scapegoat for the moral degeneracy in our nation? Even among those who do not go to that extreme, there is a large segment of citizens who want to work for stricter legal controls on objectionable materials. What should be the Christian's position on censorship?

In answering that question, all the evidence on both sides of the controversy should be considered. Then it is up to each person to decide which camp he joins, if indeed he cares one way or the other. The following is not the *only* one Christian response; it is only *one* response. With careful clarification, I basically concur with the majority recommendation of *The Report of the United States Commission on Obscenity and Pornography* as announced in the fall of 1970: "Federal, state, and local legislation prohibiting the sale, exhibition and distribution of sexual materials to consenting adults should be repealed." Advocacy of repeal must have its qualifications, as we shall see. Note now that it is not embracing pornography or advocating anarchy; rather informal social controls will accomplish the Christian's goals without the abridgment of guaranteed individual rights and the confusion of ambiguous and arbitrarily administered laws.

THE CONTROVERSIAL COMMISSION

A comment should be made about the President's Commission which was established in 1967 by President Lyndon B. Johnson. Since its release just prior to a Congressional election campaign, it very early became a popular target of political potshots. If a politician cannot be faulted for favoring home, mother, and apple pie, neither should he be attacked for being against dirty pictures and dirty books. Candidates for elective office holding those latter truths to be self-evident began climbing over each other to reach the mass media in order to express the depth of their righteous indignation against the vile recommendations of the report. President Nixon, Vice-President Agnew, and certain other politicians denounced it before they could possibly have had the time to read it. In an editorial, the *New York Times* noted these reflex denunciations and commented: "Pornography lends itself too easily to demagogic political exploitation . . . . But, over the years, the commission's calm analysis should be a useful influence in the discussion of a subject where emotionalism has ruled."[2]

A large portion of the clergy joined the fray. Many clergymen publicly concurred with Rev. Morton A. Hill, S. J., president of "Morality in Media," and the Rev. Winfrey C. Link of Hermitage, Tennessee. These commissioners began their minority report with the striking words: "The Commission's majority report is the Magna Carta for the pornographer."

Apart from the politics involved, the Christian needs to reflect seriously upon these responses. Can they create an atmosphere where others will examine the findings and interpretation with reasonable objectivity? For that matter, do we really have a deep commitment to the discovery of truth on a controversial issue, no matter how complex and difficult it is to attain or how unpleasant may be the implications? The Bible is not a gigantic, multi-volumed handbook with trillions of do's and don'ts fitting every conceivable human dilemma, big

2. *New York Times*, October 3, 1970, p. 30.

84 / OBSCENITY, PORNOGRAPHY, AND CENSORSHIP

or small. It supplies principles and demands that we discipline ourselves and apply them as carefully and honestly as we know how in our contemporary situation. This makes it essential that we look deeply at our world, our attitudes, and our own behavior. Frankly, we Christian social ethicists need all the help we can get. Nothing is to be gained and much to be lost if we engage our polemic energies in name-calling and *ad hominem* attacks. I refer to the not so new policy of labeling social scientists who investigate human sexuality as maliciously motivated, somehow mildly depraved, or bent on the destruction of our most prized Christian virtues. This rhetoric becomes a smokescreen to hide some hard truths about ourselves and our thought processes.

This is no defense of every finding of the Commission or every method of observation employed. The first people to admit the shortcomings of the Commission were the researchers who conducted it. What is defended here is the right of professionally trained investigators to approach any problem in human relations in a disciplined and scientific manner, and to labor with the assurance that the general public will have the chance to receive their findings with a grateful spirit in view of possibly adjusting its customs and laws accordingly.[3]

We shall survey four important arguments against censorship and later look at the case *for* censorship.

LEGAL AMBIGUITY

The first argument against censorship is that no law

---

3. Among the many statements, speeches, and editorials appearing in the fall of 1970, one of the most thoughtful and judicious statements to appear in a religious periodical is by Father Eugene C. Kennedy, a counseling psychologist and author, in "Kind Words for the Porno Researchers," *Commonweal*, December 18, 1970, pp. 293-94.

can be drafted so as to provide a clear and certain guide for enforcement and judicial processes. We have already discussed the three criteria offered by the Supreme Court, so there is no need for further expansion of the point; individual tastes, personal morality, customs, etc. prevent a totally objective application of these criteria. In what must be a classic admission of subjectivity, Justice Potter Stewart admitted he could not present objective legal canons but offered "I know it when I see it." This is understandable but is scarcely a legal basis for criminal indictments. Censors are people no different from ourselves; their judgments are no less fallible or open to dishonesty.

If it could be granted that the pornography user is a criminal, he is certainly a criminal with different stripes. In ordinary crime there is a victim who complains to the police and cooperates with them in apprehending the perpetrators. In moral offenses the "victim" is also the lawbreaker, and the police can enforce pornography statutes only by becoming snoopers and censors. Under such circumstances, law enforcement may begin to deteriorate and the law itself is brought into general disrespect. An analogy may be made here with the Prohibition period over forty years ago when it was finally decided that wiser public policy entailed repeal and leaving it to individuals, families, churches, and other social institutions to cope with the problem.

INSURE INDIVIDUAL RIGHTS

A second reason censorship should be abolished or greatly minimized is that the individual liberty to read and see available materials must be protected. We have established that there are many obscene, filthy, ugly, and utterly unworthy publications and films floating around, but the individual right to read and see this material must be protected for those who want it. It is not the responsibility of the law to enforce personal morals. Morality is largely a private matter. It would be both impractical and unworkable for lawmakers to legislate against, or for judges to suppress, every seemingly immoral action. Does this mean that the law is indifferent to morality? Not necessarily! The law must impose sanctions upon undeniably evil or patently dangerous activities that are so shocking that virtually all right-thinking citizens would concur they are immediately injurious to the innocent or those whose immaturity or susceptibility render them unprotected. The case against pornography is hardly that clear-cut. In fact, we are moving toward the day when all laws prohibiting any sexual behavior between consenting adults will be repealed.

Those Christians who have been the most active in declaring certain materials unfit for others to read are usually those who claim to be the most patriotic. It scarcely occurs to them that seeking to stifle the right of the people to read publications available on the open market is the type of activity generally associated with communism and totalitarian forms of government.

Take South Africa, for example—a nation with strenuous censorship laws. On the surface, authorities are merely concerned with banning works larded with sex and violence. But of the 40,000 prohibited volumes in a private Pretorian publishing firm's "Index of Objectionable Literature," one expert estimates that two-thirds of the entries were prohibited because of political content. On the list were the published works of Norman Mailer,

Martin Luther King, Harrison Salisbury, Kwame Nkrumah, Germaine Greer, and Ian Fleming.[4]

While America certainly enjoys more freedom than South Africa, we should be reminded that crimes against science, the arts, and political freedom have been committed in the name of public morality. The writings of Aristophanes, Defoe, Rousseau, and Voltaire have been seized by customs; and Hemingway, Dreiser, and Sinclair Lewis were once banned in Boston. As a nation we have matured enough so as not to repeat those mistakes. But dangerous censorship can rear its ugly head on the municipal or local level. Judith Krug and James Harvey point out that local librarians may prevent a work from reaching public readership all under the guise of sheltering the public from sexual obscenity. "Sex has become a convenient smokescreen to veil objections that have a basis less likely to gain overt public support, such as political, ideological, or racial biases."[5] The writers document this statement by naming a number of volumes that have been banned; included were Joan Baez, *Daybreak;* Stephen M. Joseph (ed.), *The Me Nobody Knows: Children's Voices from the Ghetto;* Claude Brown's *Manchild in the Promised Land;* and Eldridge Cleaver's *Soul on Ice.* These and other volumes, often giving a personal view in contemporary lingo of what it is like to grow up in America, are gladly viewed as

---

4. From AP story by Kenneth L. Whiting, *Nashville Tennessean,* March 10, 1972.
5. Judith Krug and James A. Harvey, "Intellectual Freedom," *American Libraries,* Vol. 2, (October, 1971), 1007. In the spring of 1973, the American Library Association reported more than one hundred attempts to ban books from school libraries or curricula in communities ranging from Dallas to Hollidaysburg, Pa. *Newsweek,* March 26, 1973, p. 64.

"dirty" by some. But they also accuse or argue against the "system." They tell us something has been wrong. "That moves a bigot to indignation and metamorphizes him into a censor. Censors do not read critically nor do they credit anyone else with being able to do so."[6]

New York Times critic Clive Barnes, in his introduction to the U. S. Commission Report points out that the only drama that has been prosecuted on moral grounds in the past few years has been *Che!*, written by Lennox Raphael. The play was monstrously bad—but so are many others. But the play was banned because it was also political. It attacked American policy in Cuba. The attack was confused but the political purpose of the play was always evident, says Barnes.

While the record of glamorous mistakes by censors certainly does not constitute the ultimate argument against censorship, it does underscore one fact: no legal apparatus of censorship has been devised, or probably can be devised, which is careful and subtle enough to guarantee the freedom of arts or political ideas. Granted that sexual obscenity should be curbed, can it be done in such a way that will not ill-advisedly embrace political dissent?

Take, for example, the underground newspapers written and distributed by the "New Left." There is no doubt they are filled with obscenity. So much so that most Christians may be totally repulsed by a cursory examination. Now I'm not suggesting we should cancel our subscriptions to *Time* and *Reader's Digest* and start reading the *Los Angeles Free Press* or *Berkeley Barb*. But we must remember that if dissent comes in packages that are repugnant and repulsive to our sensibilities, it is

---

6. *Ibid.*

more in the best democratic tradition and service to honor rather than ban it.[7]

A free people cannot afford to be afraid of free expression. In his dissent in the *Ginzburg v. United States* decision, Justice Potter Stewart puts the matter clearly:

> Censorship reflects a society's lack of confidence in itself. It is a hallmark of an authoritarian regime. Long ago those who wrote our First Amendment charted a different course. They believed a society can be truly strong only when it is truly free. In the realm of expression they put their faith, for better or for worse, in the enlightened choice of the people, free from the interference of a policeman's intrusive thumb or a judge's heavy hand. So it is that the Constitution protects coarse expression as well as refined, and vulgarity no less than elegance. A book worthless to me may convey something of value to my neighbor. In the free society to which our Constitution has committed us, it is for each to choose for himself.

The Christian, like the good citizen, is concerned with what grants to all men individual liberty, enlarges his access to any knowledge or new ideas, and expands the

---

7. The interested reader may wish to consult Laurence Leamer, *The Paper Revolutionaries: The Rise of the Underground Press* (New York: Simon and Schuster, 1972). It is a reasonably straightforward account of the life and times of America's underground press. With careful research in evidence, the author notes that the papers combine cultural radicalism and radical politics. Leamer believes that the underground press has covered and continues to cover material the established press refuses to or is unable to cover; in his view, these papers are the most palpable contribution of the youth culture.

opportunities for using individual decision-making and personal choice. This view liberates man rather than compresses his mind and spirit. It gives each person the privilege of enacting voluntary controls or personal discipline. As Kyle Haseldon has pointed out:

> The general rule in this area supports the need for a maximum of personal freedom and a minimum of governmental suppression. The burden of the proof in any debate between those who want man to have a maximum of freedom and those who want his access to ideas restricted should fall always on those who want to censor rather than on those who do not want knowledge and ideas censored. Freedom to receive and to utter ideas should not have to defend itself; censorship should. Freedom is always primary and privileged. Censorship should always be suspect.[8]

Emerging from these constitutional and mainly theoretical objections is another practical consideration: censorship can limit the creativity of legitimate artists. The impact of censorship on the publisher is probably nil; but the impact upon certain artists could be staggering.

Until the 1960's it is likely that we have been deprived of some writers' best work because they had to keep an eye on the law unless, of course, they were willing to limit their audience to those reached by foreign distribution or private publication. The courts

---

8. Kyle Haseldon, *Morality and the Mass Media* (Nashville, Tennessee: Broadman Press, 1968), p. 93. Haseldon, the late editor of the *Christian Century*, has much material in this useful volume that has a bearing on this subject. The book is highly recommended. Quotation used by permission of publisher.

have changed this now. The chilling effect has all but disappeared. To be practical about the whole matter, censorship in the past has not always succeeded in keeping books of literary value from being read but has only succeeded in attaching an unfortunate prurience to the reading of them. But we must not be so naive as to think all prurience will now disappear from legitimate artistic efforts, however. The problem may be more attitudinal than legal; prurience attached to reading sexually explicit materials derived less from breaking a law than from violating the social taboo which caused the law to come into existence.

NO CLEAR LINK WITH CRIMINALITY

Censorship of pornography and sexual obscenity should also be opposed because it is very difficult to demonstrate that such materials do in fact injure many people, even adolescents, severely. From any perspective, this is one of the most controversial and highly disputed issues on this question. We can only sketch the argument here and recommend further readings for those who choose to pursue it more deeply.[9]

One time Presidential adviser and Professor Daniel P. Moynihan once stated that "one particularly perverse

9. J. H. Gagnon and W. Simon (eds.), *Sexual Deviance* (New York: Harper and Row, 1967); M. Amir, *Patterns in Forcible Rape* (Chicago: University of Chicago Press, 1971); A. Bandura, *Principles of Behavior Modification* (New York: Holt, Rinehart and Winston, 1969); P. H. Gerhard, J. H. Gagnon, W. B. Pomersy, and C. V. Christenson, *Sex Offenders: An Analysis of Types* (New York: Harper and Row, 1965); L. P. Ullman and L. Krasner (eds.), *Case Studies in Behavior Modification* (New York: Holt, Rinehart and Winston, 1965); M. Hirschfeld, *Sexual Anomalies* (New York: Emerson Books, 1956).

quality of many social situations is that solutions are what may be termed 'counterintuitive.' That is, the operation of the system is such that the 'common sense' solution to a problem is very likely to be wrong."[10] Surely it is common sense to suppose that sexual crimes are caused by people who pore over pornography in their spare time. And anyone with an ounce of common sense knows that pornography will poison the minds of minors if not of adults. But common sense may, indeed, be unfounded.

Anyone wishing to establish a link between pornography and antisocial behavior will, admittedly, locate substantial circumstantial evidence and loads of opinion in both experts and non-experts. The views of the late FBI Chief J. Edgar Hoover and others of his persuasion are sprinkled liberally in various religious periodicals and church bulletin fillers.[11] Novelist Pamela H. Johnson raises some perplexing questions about the link between pornography and crime in her controversial book *On Iniquity*.[12] She questions whether the death of one small child by torture or otherwise is too high a price for "making all books available to all men."

What we must do is look at human behavior as circumspectly and objectively as we can. It may be a long time before sufficient evidence is compiled. But many researchers attempting to explore any relationship between experience with pornography and the development of normal or abnormal sexual behavior are coming to this conclusion: "Pornography cannot be shown to trigger any identifiable, specific form of sexual activity.

---

10. *Psychology Today*, September, 1970, p. 68.
11. See, for example, Hoover and others quoted in *Christianity Today*, March 18, 1966, p. 24.
12. See also Pamela H. Johnson, "Who's to Blame When a Murderer Strikes?" *Life*, August 12, 1966.

One's family background and his current attitudes—and his access to partners—seem much more likely to determine his sexual behavior."[13] Also, the rapists and child molesters observed had generally seen less pornography of all kinds than normal acting people had. A panel of psychologists at the 1970 Convention of the American Psychological Association concurred that recent studies produced little or no evidence that exposure to erotic materials had any detrimental effects on immediate character, moral values, marital behavior, or that they caused sexual deviance. One speaker reported that a brassiere ad in a national retail catalogue is more arousing than many photos of sexual intercourse.[14] As a Christian, I think it is fair to say that these psychologists have probably overstated their case. But their research and interpretations must not be sloughed off.

In his outstanding text *Abnormal Psychology and Modern Life*, James C. Coleman points out that one of the most common misconceptions about sex offenders is that they are oversexed from exposure to pornography. Instead, says Coleman, they are likely undersexed, more prudish than non-offenders, and have usually been exposed to less pornography. Coleman also states that sex offenders do not typically progress from minor to more serious sex crimes.[15]

13. Harold S. Kant and Michael J. Goldstein, "Pornography," *Psychology Today*, December, 1970, p. 59. The findings reported in this article grew out of studies done for the Commission on Obscenity and Pornography by the Legal and Behavioral Institute and were reported by the authors in recent papers before the American Sociological and Psychological Associations.
14. *New York Times*, September 8, 1970, p. 11.
15. James C. Coleman, *Abnormal Psychology and Modern Life* (4th ed.; Glenview, Illinois: Scott, Foresman, and Company, 1972), p. 463.

The most concerted effort to establish a link between pornography and sexual crime was, of course, the President's Commission with its $2,000,000 budget. The Commmission funded a number of interesting and notorious studies (one had measuring devices attached to male organs while their owners were barraged day after day with erotica). As might be expected, constant exposure to such material led to satiation and boredom. "Empirical research designed to clarify the question," declared the majority report, "has found no evidence to date that exposure to explicit sexual materials plays a significant role in the causation of delinquent or criminal behavior among youth or adults. The Commission cannot conclude that exposure to erotic materials is a factor in the causation of sex crime or sex delinquency."[16]

One bold experiment has drawn the world's attention to Denmark. After a study that involved medical, psychiatric, sociological, and church authorities, in June, 1967, Parliament voted 159 to 13 to repeal all prohibitions against written pornography. Pornographic publishers who predicted a heyday of rich profits rushed into print materials to compete on the newly legal market. But sales did not increase. More important, the increased availability of erotica has been accompanied by a decrease in the incidence of sexual crime; in 1969 there was a reported drop of 31%.[17] Any analogy made with America, however, should be carefully structured.

16. From "The Effects of Explicit Sexual Materials," *The Report of the Commission on Obscenity and Pornography* (New York: Bantam Books, 1970), pp. 26-32. The serious student should read this entire summary of research.
17. For a look at the impact of the Danes experiment as it was viewed two years later, see J. Robert Moskin's report "Legalized Pornography," *Look*, July 29, 1969, pp. 51-53.

Criminologists in Copenhagen have warned against crediting the drop in sex crime in Denmark to the famous repeal. Karl O. Christiansen, Head of Copenhagen's Criminological Institution, suggested that the ban lift had liberalized even further sex attitudes in Denmark, and the decline in reported offenses fell in areas involving public indecency, voyeurism, and male prostitution.[18]

The Christian may return to the question raised by Ms. Johnson. Should one child be tortured to death and the cause be primarily or solely attributable to pornographic sadism, would not censorship be worth this life? The question is not to be taken lightly. Certainly one life is not worth less than all the questionable books in the world. But before we legislate morality we need to make sure that one more child will really live who would not otherwise. Suppose we paid the price without absolute proof. Is it possible that we might unintentionally diminish the dimensions of life for the masses in society by restricting the artist's freedom to create or the audience's freedom to be uplifted or informed in consuming?[19]

To illustrate, a man who sees the play or movie *Fortune and Men's Eyes* (or Genet's *Chant d' amour*) which explicitly depicts the crime and disgrace of many of our penal institutions, might be moved to rape someone or become a homosexual or commit some crime so that he too can go to prison. On the other hand, he might dedicate his life and energies to greatly needed penal reform. The experience would have an effect but who can predict the effect with certainty? Sometimes

---

18. *New York Times*, January 5, 1970, p. 17.
19. See the comment by Irving Younger, "Pornography and Violence, *Nation*, August 14, 1967, p. 124.

we need to be shocked so that we will create new sensibilities and look upon the world in a new way.

OTHER CONTROLS EFFECTIVE

The final argument in the case against censorship is that there are other controls, some natural and others which must be enacted, which would be more effective in curbing the proliferation of pornography. If this point is conceded, certainly we could agree that the less power the state and police have the better our society will be.

First, anti-obscenity laws may have the effect of rendering pornography more appealing and provocative. You may remember that as an adolescent (or an adult, for that matter) there is a natural, normal curiosity in seeing pictures of the nude body. You might not have been so certain at the time that the curiosity and your response was healthy. Much like sneaking off for that first experiment with tobacco or liquor, much of the excitement of nude photos lay in the fact they were disapproved of by society or authority.

The first experience with pornography likely has a salutary effect on the curious teen-ager. Having seen what was long forbidden, he is relieved to know what it is all about. And when youth are taught that sex is dirty, says Richard Hettlinger, plastering a dormitory wall with "Playmates-of-the-Month" may serve as a medium of protest. "If we were honest enough to admit that we *all* enjoy a picture of a beautiful girl," Hettlinger admonishes fellow Christians, "there would be much less sniggering prurience and probably much less sexual deviation."[20]

---

20. Richard F. Hettlinger, *Living With Sex: The Student's Dilemma* (New York: Seabury, 1966), p. 38.

Censorship laws then, besides being of questionable legality and enforcement, serve to make pornography more alluring, especially to those with a special bent against being bossed in their personal lives or who think they need the luxury of being naughty every once in a while. Herbert Gold, writing in the *Saturday Review*, states that the very lifeblood of the pornographic publisher depends on an air of illegality. He makes his point vividly: the pornographer "depends on repression, and now must function out in the open, with insufficient persecution by the state. How would you feel if you had ambitions to be a rapist and all the girls cried 'Try me! me!'?"[21] Pamela Johnson offers a tongue-in-cheek recommendation that all plays be performed in stark nakedness for a month "so that we might get this particular silliness out of our systems."[22]

Second, the eventual boredom that pornography evokes in most people will restore the needed balance. This does not mean that sex will disappear from the scene as a theme for novels, plays, and movies. God forbid! But distorted, impoverished, masturbatory approaches to erotic themes in the media will diminish as the general public gets bored with the whole thing. The long refusal to permit totally honest treatment of sexual themes in the media has conditioned a nation of voyeurs. Now that the dust of controversy is settling, there already seems to be a boredom, a fed-up-ness, with the exploitation of sex in the media.

In the movie industry there is no doubt that the pendulum has begun to swing the other way. No longer

21. Herbert Gold, "The End of Pornography," *Saturday Review*, October 31, 1970, p. 25.
22. "Peddling the Pornography of Violence," *Encounter*, February, 1970, p. 74.

can a film that touts explicit scenes be guaranteed a large audience. When *I Am Curious—Yellow* stirred up such a legal hassle in America in 1969, the result was incredibly long lines of people waiting to pay up to $5.00 a ticket to see what, by almost any critic, was a monstrously bad movie. Anticipating another killing before American audiences, the producers rushed stateside a sequel *I Am Curious—Blue,* equally bad, but this time there were no long lines. Both boredom and a lost excitement of the forbidden meant those long lines were not to be "turned on" again.

Third, the banning of censorship does not preclude the functioning of institutional controls. The home is the basic unit of society and where else might control be more effective? Parochial schools and private colleges, and to a lesser extent the public schools and colleges, retain the freedom to legislate the kind of ideas and entertainment to which students will be exposed. Denominational bodies can draft guidelines to be used and adapted by local congregations according to their own needs and situations. More will be said about this later.

Fourth, the mass communication media can cut excesses through industry self-regulation. Self-imposed codes have been effective in the comic book, radio and television and motion picture industries, and citizen support for regulation should render these efforts even more effective.

Finally, since pornography is used to satisfy a natural interest in sex, interest in it would dwindle if adolescents had access to adequate information regarding sex offered through appropriate sex education. In most cases, the principal source of sex information for youngsters remains their peers; parents, church, and physicians are not significant sources; schools, however, are a much more important source today than a generation ago. A wide number of sex education programs have been initiated in recent years and in a short time empirical studies should be completed enabling evaluation and adaptation for future efforts.

This is not intended as an unqualified defense of every sex education program that has been initiated. But the simple fact is that many young people, in spite of efforts at sophistication, are woefully ignorant of some basic information about sex.[23] Regrettably, some of the strongest opposition to sex education in the public schools has come from conservative Christians. Somehow there is the belief that knowledge about sex *ipso facto* leads to sexual immorality. In reality, what we have is an admission of our own failures and lack of persuasiveness in teaching the moral standards that must responsibly direct this newly discovered knowledge. So long as existing means of sex education are undesirable and/or inadequate, positive attitudes and values in sexuality become the responsibility of *both* the schools and the home, the latter with the help of the church. Shirking the responsibility of adequate sex education leaves a void that we may be asking pornography to fill.

Could there be other natural forces at work that will coalesce to retard the spread of smut? Critic Stanley Kauffman believes there are. He writes:

> The growing realizations about the historic mistreatment of women, some new aspects of community, the thorough reexamination of social values generally, some understanding of the interplay of money and sex, the growing

---

23. This point was made clear in a special cover story about teen-age sexual behavior in *Time*, August 21, 1972, p. 35.

hungers for moral honesty—all these forces
which are now evident in our society, though
hardly yet triumphant, are the real enemies of
pornography.[24]

We may hope that Kauffmann is correct. Regardless,
there are some positive actions that Christians may take,
as we shall see later.

IS THERE ANY GOOD TO BE SAID ABOUT
PORNOGRAPHY?

I have not exhausted all the arguments against censorship of sexual obscenity. Four others can be mentioned
but I do not consider them particularly persuasive.

First, if there is an intense (and profitable) demand
for pornography, there will always be an adequate supply no matter how severe the legal penalties. This by
itself is not sufficient grounds for banning censorship.
There will always be criminals in certain areas (for
example, tax evasion or drunken driving), but the fact
that crime is far from abolished in a given area is no
argument for lifting legal controls; instead, it may call
for tougher enforcement.

Second, it is argued that pornography can be a valuable source of sex education for young people. The
President's Commission discovered that for about 50%
of both sexes, sexually explicit materials were a significant factor in learning about sex.[25] Granted that such
materials could be helpful, no *prima facie* case for
pornography could be established on this point alone.

24. Stanley Kauffman, "On Obscenity," *The New Republic*, October 17, 1970, p. 35.
25. *U. S. Commission*, pp. 314-16.

But it would be a mistake to believe that sexually-exploitative materials free anyone from crippling inhibitions and promotes healthy attitudes toward sexuality. Conversely, they may deposit ugly images and distorted conceptions in the consciousness or subconsciousness of our youth, a point raised earlier.

Third, it is argued that pornography can serve as an aphrodisiac for married couples who need "new life" in their sexual relationship. How hard-core pornography "turns on" a normal couple that cannot otherwise be excited is beyond this writer. A marriage that is held afloat only by pornography is truly in trouble. And a marriage that depends on such external stimulation will likely find the law of diminishing returns catching up with them.

Finally, it is arguable that some people are rendered socially less dangerous by having their sexual tensions and frustrations satisfied by pornography, unrelieved tensions would well up into antisocial or criminal acts. This is called the "drain-off" or "catharsis" theory. This point is made by Abraham Kaplan in his essay "Obscenity as an Esthetic Category."[26] Kaplan argued that what he called "Dionysian obscenity" not only was not necessarily immoral but served as a moral agent; by providing a catharsis or sublimation, this kind of art serves as a "safety-valve" without which libidinal pressures may explode.

This thesis has been given a more recent plug for the readership of *Saturday Review*. In an essay defending even the worst of hard-core pornography, "For a Volup-

----

26. Printed from a symposium "Obscenity and the Arts," appearing in *Law and Contemporary Problems* (Vol. 20, No. 4, Autumn, 1955), published by Duke University School of Law.

tuous Tomorrow," the celebrated French novelist, film-maker, and literary critic, Alain Robbe-Grillet pleads "let us not judge according to morality, but with pragmatism and a little good faith. What harm does it do—to anyone—if the customer with sadistic tastes . . . lingers over [pornography mixing sadistic violence with nudity] such images?"[27] Commenting on one of the pornography centers of the world, the Frenchman adds:

> The bookshops on 42nd Street are not an academy of sadistic murder and "unnatural" fornication. Rather, such places are a kind of great national theatre of our passions, more or less excessive, more or less specialized, but indeed the passions of this society. And it is in such places, provided we are eighteen or over, that we can at last contemplate quite openly our hidden faces, thereby transforming into freedom, play, and pleasure what was merely alienation and risked becoming crime and madness.[28]

Robbe-Grillet reminds us of mathematician Henri Poincaré's remark that "an adult needs pornography as a child needs fairy tales."

This theory is at complete odds with the one that says such obscenity *causes* antisocial or criminal behavior and, quite frankly, is just as unsubstantiated. If we were to grant that some people need pornography it is probably true that they need a psychiatrist even more. Still, since many are unlikely to seek out professional help maybe the existence of some pornography can be a substitute.

---

27. *Saturday Review,* May 20, 1972, p. 46.
28. *Ibid.*

One warning: we need to be certain that the term "catharsis" is not employed as a blank check endorsement of every form of media mayhem. The "catharsis" idea can be carried to the point of *reductio ad absurdum.* Aristotle never meant it that way. Do parents give their children a coloring book to rid them of a natural interest in art or painting? Is the son given an erector set to eradicate any interest in real construction or toy trains and autos so that he will seek other means of transportation? Is the daughter given a toy typewriter so she will not later seek out secretarial employment? Should a son be given a chemistry set to erase a natural bent for science or a small football to make sure he doesn't develop the desire to play ball professionally when he is older? To answer affirmatively would be absurd. This is not debunking the catharsis theory but merely guarding against building a case for pornography solely on its basis.

QUALIFYING THE CENSORSHIP BAN

A total ban of censorship is not advocated without qualifications. Restrictions are, for the most part, already established in most communities. What may be stressed here is the importance of tough enforcement by severe penalties.

(1) Any store selling or specializing in pornographic materials must be licensed and subject to full taxation.

(2) Signs should be posted near the entrance to warn an unsuspecting public. Window displays of the wares sold should not be allowed. Public tastes and sensibilities must be respected.

(3) No advertising should be permitted in regular newspapers or other media. A few city newspapers have already begun the policy of refusing advertising for

X-rated or sexploitation films; this lead should be followed elsewhere. (4) Sales should be made only to adults who seek out such business establishments. (5) Absolutely no soliciting and selling of materials to minors. This means there shall be no sending or soliciting for pornography through the mails, simply because children and/or unsuspecting adults are likely to be involved. The last two points are important and worthy of further elaboration.

For generations the state and society have correctly established laws based on the fundamental difference between the almost boundless individual freedom of adults and the protection that is the innate right of children. The responsible society will provide the best possible climate for the struggle by its youth to develop stable and meaningful patterns of interpersonal behavior. Pornography, either hard-core or in its more sophisticated forms, may serve only to confuse and bewilder children who are exposed to it. The maturing of children along wholesome lines is in serious danger when their conceptions of the purpose, nature, and values of sexuality are distorted; the formation of sound adult relationships in the future may be jeopardized.

Several authorities have stressed the importance of restraint and delay in the sexual responses of youth. In an article entitled "Why I Dislike Western Civilization," historian Arnold Toynbee argues that a culture which postpones rather than stimulates sexual experience in young adults is a culture most prone to progress.[29] Margaret Mead puts it this way:

---

29. *New York Times Magazine*, May 10, 1964, pp. 15+.

Every society has the task of bringing up children who will focus their capacities for sexual feeling on particular persons, with or without overt bodily expression, and who will not only refrain from large amounts of undirected, objectless sex behavior, but will be able to produce the proper intensity of feeling expressed or unexpressed for the proper object.[30]

Drawing a line that insures the right of every adult to read or see whatever he desires but that also does not expose the minor to materials that might have a detrimental effect on his emotional development is the challenge with which legislators are faced. The line is not always easy to draw; there may be some overlapping of exigencies. Christians should support this basic rule: *the greater the medium's exposure to minors, the more justified the government is in imposing restraints on the content and manner of presentation.* This suggests that our present policy of placing the more stringent controls upon the television medium is justified.

In conclusion, society's most precious and important possession is its children. The responsibility of equipping them for mature and responsible adulthood has never been easy. The new freedom enjoyed by the mass media has served only to compound that problem. Parents should remember that the handling of contemporary tension lies not with any one institution; in descending order of importance, the home, the church, the school, and, much further down the line, the government share the responsibility. In discharging this responsibility, all our errors—if any—should be on the side of

---

30. Quoted in Kuh, *Foolish Fig-leaves*, pp. 240-41.

restraint and caution. If there is tension between the freedom of adults to consume pornography and the rights of children not to be confronted with it, the conflict must always be resolved in favor of the children. This seems the prudent course. Then when juveniles mature into adulthood they may make their own decisions as to whether they want to exploit or be exploited. If children while under the stewardship of Christian parents are taught and shown a fundamental respect for other people and encouraged in a psychological and moral discipline, they shall surely make the right decision.

QUESTIONS FOR DISCUSSION

1. Why do you think people take pride in refusing to be shocked? Do you agree with the author that most people who advocate censorship intend it to be used against others?
2. Do you agree that Christian social ethicists should rely heavily on the findings and theories of social scientists (sociologists, social psychologists, psychiatrists, etc.) in making biblical principles relevant to our contemporary situation?
3. Do you believe that all laws prohibiting any sexual behavior (whether normal or deviant) between consenting adults should be repealed?
4. Do the writings of New Left and black radicals serve a positive function in our democratic society?
5. If pornography could be definitely proven to cause sex crimes, could not legitimate artistic works treating sexual themes have the very same effect?
6. Does forbidding any experience make it more attractive to adolescents?
7. Can the appeal of pornography be reduced by thorough sex education?
8. Even if pornography does inadvertently provide some sex education, why must children be protected from seeing it?

6

The Case for Censorship

Controlling the content and manner of communication is a human necessity and a social inevitability. In broad terms, the question is not: to censor or not to censor. The question is how much and in what ways to censor, who is delegated the authority to censor, and for what specific purposes censorship should be employed. In this study the term "censorship" has been used in the limited sense of formal, governmental control and we have outlined a case against this form of censorship, keeping in mind certain other restrictions.

On the other hand, a persuasive case can be made for tougher governmental controls on pornography and obscenity. The issue is too important for Christians to see only one side, so the other approach is acknowledged here. I think it is fair to say that those responsible critics who call for tougher censorship laws are not necessarily more concerned or more righteous. In terms of American tradition they certainly are more conservative. Most critics calling for censorship bans and those arguing for tighter public controls are in fundamental agreement on opposition to pornography and needless obscenity in the media, but disagree as to the methods of diminishing the menace.

All that will be done here is explain the basic arguments. For further reading of arguments by attorneys and professors who favor tougher censorship laws, the following should be examined: Political Scientist Harry Clor, *Obscenity and Public Morality* (University of Chicago Press, 1969), and Attorney Richard H. Kuh, *Foolish Figleaves? Pornography in and out of Court* (Macmillan Company, 1967). There are several briefer studies or essays. Three are recommended: Political Scientist Reo M. Christenson, "Censorship of Pornography? Yes," *The Progressive*, September, 1970; Walter Berns, "Pornography vs. Democracy," *The Public Interest*, Winter, 1971; and Professor of Urban Values Irving Kristol, "Pornography, Obscenity, and the Case for Censorship," *New York Times Magazine*, March 28, 1971. Walter Berns, *Freedom, Virtue, and the First Amendment* (Greenwood, 1957) is also highly recommended.

There are two major, related philosophical arguments in support of tougher censorship of pornography: (1) No individual is granted complete freedom and the law is justified in imposing greater restraints even on individual, adult behavior when his decisions are deemed harmful to himself; and (2) Laws, even if unenforced or without unanimous support, should exist as sanctions guiding and protecting the general public morality.

FIRST AMENDMENT NOT ABSOLUTE

One myth that is prone to gain popular acceptance in America is that an individual is free to do anything he likes so long as his action does not have any undesirable effect on any other person or group of persons. But the bald fact is that none of us can be an unequivocal, uncompromised civil libertarian. There are at least a very few limitations the government may put on human behavior even if the consequences are not contagious. Why is this true? Simply because it does not follow that just because a man wants to do something it is good for him—or at worst only a harmless diversion—and society is within its rights in acting on its belief that it is not, especially in the absence of proof to the contrary. There are several instances in which the law is paternalistic. Take narcotics, for example. The law is designed to protect the individual against the harmful effects of narcotics and drug abuse. Like it or not, the law compels the workingman to put away funds for the future of himself and his fellow citizens (Social Security), and with many types of employment there are safety regulations with which the worker must comply (e.g., in mining, construction, welding, etc.). Gambling and prostitution are still illegal in most places, though many a person has insisted he was harmed by neither. Most states have laws making it mandatory for motorcyclists to wear or carry crash helmets and have other safety equipment, and the day may be coming when there may be a federal law requiring automobile passengers to use seat belts while riding.

Now the question is, where do we draw the line? Where are the limits of individual freedom? At what point should police step in to prohibit the "self-expression" of some performer or group, even when what is going on is between "consenting adults" and is intended as artistic expression? It is not wholly unthinkable in an age when weird and eccentric types easily engage the attention of the media that, should a movie producer or play director call for an actor to commit suicide on the set or stage to enhance the impact of "realism," somebody just might step forward and volunteer for the part.

Of course that would not be allowed. Nor would we allow some willing masochist to be tortured by scourging and mutilation even if it did heighten the effect. And even if some free-spirited millionaire were to demand and finance it, no right-thinking law official would permit a resurrection of the old Roman gladiatorial games in Houston's Astrodome—even with a stipulation that only consenting adults be involved.

The point is, as emphasized by Berns and Kristol, that no society can afford to be utterly indifferent to the ways its citizens publicly entertain themselves. Bearbaiting and cockfighting are outlawed only in part because of humane compassion for innocent, suffering animals. The most important reason such entertainment forms were abolished was because they debased, brutalized, and hardened the folks who gathered to witness such spectacles. Since pornography—especially performed pornography—is just as debasing and brutally destructive of human relationships, it too should be outlawed.

Of course the constitutional consideration is what was meant by the First Amendment: "Congress shall make no law . . . abridging freedom of speech or press." Is the "no law" absolute and without exception, as in the view of Justices William Douglas and Hugo Black, or does the amendment need more qualification? The moralist and the libertarian approach the First Amendment with differing and often sharply conflicting basic premises. The libertarian will usually bring to his interpretation of the First Amendment freedoms a conception (explicit or implicit) of the primacy of individual freedom in our political and constitutional order. This is the view of the American Civil Liberties Union. Libertarians do not advocate the unlimited right to say anything, anywhere, and in any manner. Their position does assert, at least, that the right to speak shall never hinge upon a weighing of the values to be attained by restriction against the *quality* or *content* of the speech to be restricted.

The moralist is sometimes compelled to deny the doctrine of the primacy of individual freedom.[1] He will argue that it is not just the freedom to do as we please, but "rational freedom" or "true freedom" which is the ultimate goal of our political order. To the moralist, some forms of limitation or qualification upon the First Amendment are simply inherent in the exigencies of social life. "Human freedoms are essentially subordinated to good morals and are safeguarded by them," states Monsignor Thomas J. Fitzgerald. "A campaign for good morals is not an infringement upon freedom, but a preparation for the enjoyment of true freedom."[2] Further, the moralist might rightfully insist that his presuppositions about the First Amendment do more to promote genuine democracy than the premises of the libertarian; there is an antidemocratic strain in the libertarians' ideology because of their unwillingness to permit the citizenry at large to employ legislative process to cope with a social problem.[3]

---

1. For a persuasive argument against the belief that freedom is, or can be, the first principle of our political order, see Walter Berns, *Freedom, Virtue, and the First Amendment* (Westport, Conn: Greenwood, 1957).
2. Quoted in Harold C. Gardiner, *Catholic Viewpoint on Censorship* (Garden City, New York: Doubleday, 1961), pp. 187-88. For another Catholic view on censorship, see Rev. John J. Regan, "The Supreme Court and Obscenity," *Vital Speeches,* 31 (July 15, 1965), 592-95.
3. For a defense of censorship based on the "majoritarian" argument, see Terence J. Murphy, *Censorship: Government and Obscenity* (Baltimore: Helicon, 1963), pp. 120-21.

Most libertarian Supreme Court justices have advocated some limits to "free speech" as guaranteed by the Bill of Rights. You have probably heard of the term "clear and present danger," a limitation voiced by Oliver Wendell Holmes in *Schenck v. United States* (1919). Some of the laws that have abridged free expression have dealt with libel, perjury, incitement to violence, contempt of court, disrespect toward command officers, copyright violation, and violation of local laws concerning time and place of assembly. The First Amendment itself has a built-in limitation on free speech; by implication, the "establishment of religion" clause precludes the indoctrination of religious dogma in public, tax-supported schools. Some of the most restrictive laws on free expression were passed in the early decades of this republic.

Let's illustrate this by looking again at one First Amendment liberty. The First Amendment forbids the Congress to pass any law "prohibiting the free exercise" of religion. And yet, polygamy has been made a crime despite the fact that it historically has been a major tenet of a recognized religion.[4] Why is it that the prohibition of polygamy is not deemed the "prohibition" which the First Amendment forbids? The reason: an overriding public purpose. Not to outlaw polygamy was perceived as setting in order consequences that would undermine the perservation of our family structure on which our society rests.

What did the founding fathers mean by this amendment?[5] It is often asserted that the libertarian views of Justices Black and Douglas have adequate support not

---

4. *Reynolds v. United States*, 98 U. S. 145 (1879).
5. For an excellent discussion of this topic see Clor, *Obscenity and Public Morality*, pp. 94-103.

only in the constitutional text but in the views and intentions of the very men who drafted this document. James Madison's strongest and most specific exposition about the meaning of the First Amendment was written during the controversy over the Alien and Sedition Acts; and Thomas Jefferson expressed virtually the same views in his *Kentucky Resolutions.* Passages from Madison and Jefferson can be ushered in that assert in unequivocal terms the absoluteness of speech and press freedoms. What is often forgotten, however, is that the specific context in which they speak is political. The restraints condemned are on political criticism.

In answer to the above question, the best explanation is that Congress may place no *unreasonable* restraints on free expression. The framers of our constitution most likely intended no absolute ban on governmental intervention in the dissemination of political, religious, social, and economic views. Despite the fact that civil libertarians purport to find in the words of the First Amendment the simple and easy answer to this complex problem, the founding fathers apparently did not address themselves to obscenity and pornography.

The crux of the legal battle is simply this: Does a totally obscene play, movie, or dance enjoy the protection of the First Amendment? It cannot be denied that motion pictures, plays, and the like are significant media for the communication of ideas. They may affect public attitudes and behavior in a variety of ways, ranging from explicit statement to the subtle shaping of thought which characterizes most artistic expression. But what about some publication or production that seems totally worthless and totally irrelevant to democratic political process?

The view that is gaining wider legal acceptance is that

such obvious obscenity enjoys legal protection. The rationale is twofold: first, the line between the inform-ing and the entertaining functions of media is too elu-sive and courts must therefore cast a wide net over all forms of communication in order to protect that which is of potential political or social relevance; and second, the life of the imagination and intellect is of comparable import to the preservation of the political process and so the First Amendment must reach beyond govern-mental-citizenry affairs and in addition protect the in-terest in free interchange of ideas and impressions for their own sake, for whatever gain the individual may derive.[6] Thus, the constitution protects all forms of communication, from the highest (the work of art) to the basest.

Those arguing for stronger censorship laws support another interpretation. The right to advocate the most repulsive forms of sexual perversion enjoys full legal protection only so long as the proponent is clearly attempting to persuade rather than to entertain com-mercially. Commercial public entertainment cannot en-joy the same legal privileges as political discourse.

What if the two forms are combined? The greater the moral suasion and the less of entertainment, the more such efforts must be protected. But, as Christenson points out, no one has yet to prove that effective

6. Morris Ernst has often expressed the idea that no distinction can be permitted between education and entertainment—they both equally belong to the realm of ideas for ideas' sake and judgments of the goodness or badness of an idea seem to be a matter for "the whims of a passing generation." Professor Alexander Meiklejohn in his *Political Freedom* (Harper and Row, 1948 and 1960), on the other hand, makes a distinction between all speech about "public issues" (protected abso-lutely) and speech directed toward our private interests and needs (qualified protection from the Due Process Clause).

dissemination of viewpoints demands the use of porno-graphic techniques. A *reductio ad absurdum* may crys-tallize the viewpoint: some poor fellow arrested for indecent exposure on the downtown square may insist his exhibitionism was his effort at protesting poverty (and maybe he is right) but few would insist this kind of "message" is permissible. Any loss of free expression that occurs with sensible pornography legislation is only marginal and more than adequately compensated by the accrued benefits of protected citizens and improved social environment, it may be argued.

LAWS SERVE HORTATORY AND SYMBOLIC FUNCTION

Related to the first objection is another key argument in favor of tougher anti-pornography and obscenity leg-islation. It runs as follows: public opinion polls reveal that the majority of Americans favor tougher controls on pornography. The great "silent majority" of Ameri-cans, a term enjoying wide use since Nixon assumed the Presidency, are affronted by the spread of vulgarity and by intuition entertain a long-ingrained suspicion that all of this will eventually undermine moral restraints essen-tial to this nation's greatness. And until more convincing scientific proof is available to convince the majority of citizens that their fears are ill-founded, majority views should prevail. Put simply, if the majority thinks censor-ship guards the quality of American life, the laws need to be on the books.

The purpose of such laws need not be understood as an effort by the government to distract men's interest from the carnal or sensual aspects of life and serve the more noble and spiritual matters. The censorship would not aim at directing thoughts *anywhere*. Instead, its purpose would be to control some of those forces in our modern mass society which operate to lower moral standards and, ultimately, debase moral character. If the influences which debase moral character are restrained, the possibility for the emergence and development of truly worthy thoughts and ideals is greatly enhanced.

This view of the moral purpose of law is not new. It is rooted in Aristotelian philosophy. Aristotle believed that men did not form political societies simply for the preservation of life, liberty, and security, but to promote the whole range of human needs, both the material (or "lower") as well as the moral (or "higher") needs. Lawmakers were to make citizens good by training them in habits of right action. Certainly society existed to preserve life but its highest end was the good life—the development in citizens of those qualities and capacities which are uniquely human. Individual offenders of what appears to be man's uniquely human integrity and responsibility are controlled and directed by authoritative guidance and encouragement from the political community through the legal process.

Walter Berns accepts this classical view. To him, the public and private morality of a community is dependent on developing and maintaining citizens of a certain character and, consequently, it must be the task of the law to promote such a character. Hence, "the formation of character is the principal duty of government."[7]

Stiffer laws, then, would serve as sanctions guarding the general morality and also serve as symbols of majority views. Controls or censorship arises from a felt need, whatever its purpose, for unity or cohesion. The very

---

7. Berns, *Freedom, Virtue, and the First Amendment*, p. 246.

term "community" presupposes common values and beliefs which bind its members together and promote common allegiances and actions. The ideals, virtues, and values the law supports may be good or may be bad when judged in light of some ideal, universal standard of human excellence. But that is not the point. The important matter is not the intrinsic merit and validity of various tenets in a community's political, social, and moral ideologies but the role of the law in preserving and protecting these tenets upon which the survival of the community is based.[8]

Clor also concurs with this view. To him, the preventive and coercive functions of governmental censorship are supplemented, and perhaps superseded, by its hortatory and educative functions.[9] Censorship laws proclaim that the organized community draws a line between art and pornography, the decent and the indecent, the permissible and the not permissible. Exploiters may indeed step over the line, but at least they are fully aware that a line exists and this awareness cannot but have a positive effect upon the moral attitudes and values of most people.

It might be argued that censorship laws cannot be enforced evenly or effectively. To the moralist, this objection is hardly material so long as the majority favor the law. The laws remain on the books as legal endorsement for the popular basis of general morality. Prohibition was not enforced effectively either, liberals argue.

---

8. For a discussion of this point and a contemporary critique of John Stuart Mill, see Patrick Devlin, *The Enforcement of Morals* (London: Oxford University Press, 1959). See also H. L. A. Hart, *Law, Liberty, and Morality* (Stanford: Stanford University Press, 1965).
9. Clor, *Obscenity and Public Morality*, p. 194.

The difference, moralists answer, lies in the fact that the Prohibition Amendment was pushed through by a propagandizing, vocal minority while the majority was generally opposed or at best passive and indifferent to the issue. The Prohibition Amendment was the greatest short-term legislative success of our Protestant churches, but it turned out to be an abysmal long-range failure. The reason: fundamentalist and conservative Protestants were attempting to impose their moral convictions on Roman Catholics, Jews, and liberal Protestants, not to mention the unaffiliated. Certainly churches should attempt to raise the general level of public morality and to sensitize people to moral issues where they are currently uninformed or apathetic. But, as Christian ethicist John C. Bennett warns, churches must acknowledge the limits of law as the means for regulation of the day-by-day personal behavior of citizens.[10]

Laying utopian visions of society aside, the law must deal with social reality. And, paradoxically, the existence of some censorship may serve to insure greater freedom. When law is too far ahead of the average citizen, the average citizen may take the law into his own hands. In the past, a decline in governmental censorship has led to an increase in private vigilantism—a disrespectable and uncivilized manner of handling social problems, but a reality just the same.[11]

---

10. John C. Bennett, "Church and State," *New Frontiers of Christianity*, ed. Ralph C. Raughley, Jr. (New York: Association Press, 1962), pp. 188-93.
11. Morris Ernst reports: "The great irony, however, is that while courts are restricting the powers of government in the field of so-called obscenity, the 'vigilantism' or private groups is on the increase. By 'vigilantism,' here, we are referring to all forms of essentially private pressure attempting to regulate what we read and see." *Censorship: The Search for the Obscene*, pp. 233-34.

Professor Oliver Wendell Holmes, Jr., of Harvard Law School, once addressed himself to this point. "The first requirement of a sound body of law," he asserts, "is that it should correspond with the actual feelings and demands of the community, *whether right or wrong.* If people would gratify the passion of revenge outside the law, if the law did not help them, the law has no choice but to satisfy the craving itself, and thus avoid the greater evil of private retribution."[12] In any case, while laws tend to make pornography appear as "forbidden fruit," total repeal would not eliminate the general public's disapproval or any attacked stigma; for such a stigma stems more from public opinion on obscenity than any law restricting it.

Briefly, two things may be said in evaluation of this second main argument for stricter controls. First, while most citizens are opposed to pornography, it is doubtful the intensity of their opposition in the 1970's is such to justify laws passed symbolically or to prevent vigilantism. Second, unsupported and unenforced laws encourage disrespect for law, especially among the youth.

The negative effect on the integrity and reputation of the law comes from several factors. Laws safeguarding "public morality" tend to be vaguely defined. Such vagueness is the source of official uncertainty and often leads to variable and arbitrary enforcement. Offenses are typically "crimes without victims."[13] With the absence of victims and the relatively private nature of the proscribed activity, police have additional problems; with-

---

12. *The Common Law* (1881), 41-42.
13. See Edwin M. Schur, *Crimes Without Victims* (Englewood Cliffs, New Jersey: Prentice-Hall, 1965). Also see Richard J. Neuhaus, "Sense and Nonsense About Victimless Crimes," *Christian Century*, March 7, 1973, pp. 281-85.

out the assistance of complainants, enforcement officers feel they must exercise active surveillance over the community. This situation is no deterrent to the problems of illegal search and seizure, provocation and harassment.[14]

When nonconformists are branded as criminals—whether justly or not—the law tends to cast them apart from the legitimate community. Even if a person believes the proscribed activity is not intrinsically immoral (by whatever standard), the atmosphere of secrecy, suspicion, and deviousness that must accompany it comes to have its own degrading effect. And what begins as a minor or limited deviation from society's norms may grow into a new life style, especially when the deviant comes to depend on criminal sources who supply the illicit goods or services. To the suppliers of contraband commodities, legal prohibitions create a bonanza, affording new opportunities for exploitation and profit they would not otherwise have. In this sense, the legal enactment creates criminals.[15]

Proponents of censorship admit that a long list of worthwhile and even exceptionally outstanding works of literary art have been banned in the past. In *The Censor Marches On*, Morris Ernst and Alexander Lindsey present a four-page listing of works banned during the last three thousand years. A closer examination may render these lists less impressive, especially when one asks "Who did the banning?" and "How extensive was

---

14. See Jerome H. Skolnick, *Justice Without Trial* (New York: Wiley, 1966), pp. 204-29.
15. See Herbert L. Packer, "The Crime Tariff," *The American Scholar*, 33 (1964), 551-57, and Francis A. Allen, *The Borderland of Criminal Justice* (Chicago: University of Chicago Press, 1964).

the ban?" But even if the lists were taken at face value, moralists argue, the people denied exposure to these works of art were not rendered significantly less intelligent or mature as a result. Nor did a fever of censorship spread to all other areas of art and learning. Clor points out that while Victorian sex censorship in England was not confined to worthless obscenity (it reached into most areas of literary, poetic, and dramatic expression involving sex), still there was an ever widening toleration for criticism and unorthodoxy in matters of religion and politics.[16] In fact censorship in one area of life may unconsciously serve to provide some aspect of life with certainty and stability in the midst of doubt and revolution in other areas. And while a work of artistic value may be delayed in publication by stricter censorship, it would ultimately be vindicated.

One thing both civil libertarians and moralists share in this controversy is a strong distaste for the kind of presentation of sex and/or violence whose sole purpose is to shock and offend. Under the conditions of cultural pluralism that exist in America, when the law enters the area of sexual morality, there is consensus that it may clash with the beliefs and aspirations of substantial minorities; this produces the necessity for liberty. But couldn't all right-thinking citizens—regardless of religious, ethnic, or political group membership—concur that presentations intended solely to shock or offend must be banned?

This view received a strong endorsement in 1970 by Dr. Benjamin Spock, long considered an authority on child care and hardly a typical book-burning zealot.

---

16. *Obscenity and Public Morality*, p. 115. Normal St. John-Stevas in *Obscenity and the Law* (New York: Macmillan Co., 1956), p. 29 makes the same point.

Spock says that evidence linking pornography with anti-social criminal behavior (or lack of same) is quite beside the point. Movies, plays, novels, articles, and paintings in which the primary aim is to shock, revolt, or embarrass through stark explicitness of sexual intimacies—especially those of a loveless, perverse, or brutal kind—have no redeeming value and should be banned. Spock says that even sincere efforts to shield children often fail and the lack of new censorship laws seems less risky "when a society already has soaring rates of delinquency and crime, an insatiable appetite for brutality on television and what I consider an unprecedented loss of belief in man's worthiness."[17]

Still, many libertarians will not concur with Spock's solution. Shock is a transitory phenomenon, they argue, that occurs usually only upon first exposure to previously forbidden material. Consequently, what is considered shocking and what is commonplace varies from age to age, generation to generation, and maybe even from year to year. Since shock survives best in an atmosphere of suppression, the best protection against it is exposure. Further, this overlooks the probability that at times our sensibilities deserve to be shocked. Liberals argue that while loveless, tasteless, and perverse sado-masochistic trash exists, it is part of the price we pay for revering and safeguarding the First Amendment. And so the debate continues on and on. What should be clear by now is that there can be no stance toward the question of censoring obscenity and pornography which

---

17. Benjamin Spock, "A Reactionary View of Obscenity and Brutality," *Redbook*, January, 1970, pp. 20 and 22. The article reproduced excerpts from his book *Decent and Indecent: Our Personal and Political Behavior.*

does not involve certain moral, political, social, and psychological premises.

Looking to the future the concerned Christian will want to keep an open mind on the issue, examine new arguments, evidence, or interpretation, and then act accordingly. But the question of accepting the legal situation for what it is today or agitating for stricter governmental controls seems to be more academic than practical. One reason, as should be quite clear by now, is that official censorship is not the sole or most effective means of control. But the second, and equally important reason, is that the most dangerous and destructive forms of obscenity and pornography, at least from the Christian viewpoint, will not be touched by censorship laws. It is to that consideration that we turn next.

QUESTIONS FOR DISCUSSION

1. Do you think that people who are opposed to governmental censorship are "soft" on pornography and public immorality?
2. What is meant by the statement that the law is paternalistic? Do you agree that it should be?
3. Why is the First Amendment guarantee of freedom of speech not absolute?
4. What did the founding fathers probably mean by "freedom of speech"?
5. Can one determine when a public expression is political in nature or primarily entertainment?
6. Is there a value in having a law that is difficult to enforce?
7. Why did the Prohibition movement among Protestant churches turn out to be a long-range failure?
8. Do you agree that shock survives best in an atmosphere of suppression, and the best protection against it is exposure?

7

Expanding the Christian Concept of Pornography

Most of our discussion thus far has centered around what is usually called "hard-core" pornography or sexual obscenity. Hard-core materials dramatize the pornography problem in its most offensive and feared forms; moralists have long referred to such materials as the "sewers," "gutters," or "cesspools" of society. But our labels and the fears they create may only serve to obscure another important aspect of the problem that will be explored in the following two chapters.

Sexual morality is interpersonal in nature. The repudiation of the personal dimension is the fundamental earmark of sexual immorality. The greater the denial, the greater the immorality. This denial may be crudely explicit or subtly implicit. A prostitute who rents her body to a willing customer has reduced sexuality to a totally depersonalized and marketable item. The men and women who rent their bodies for journalistic exploitation would be in the same category. But a more frequent denial of the personal dimension in human sexuality is implicitly imposed upon the American people. You do not have to go to a dirty book store or attend a sexploitation movie to be exposed to pornography in some form.

We have already explained that pornography is

known by its fruits, or effects. It exploits, invades privacy and individuality, erodes Christian attitudes, and represents sexuality in a dishonest manner. If a careful observer uses the "effects" criteria for defining and locating pornography, he can come to only one conclusion—hard-core pornography composes only a small percentage of all the objectionable behavior and materials in the media today. The more damaging kind of obscenity is frequently called "soft-core" or "pious pornography."

If hard-core materials are more dangerous to spiritual development, it is only because they more flagrantly and more obviously exploit, depersonalize, and treat sex dishonestly. But everyone recognizes it for what it is. Not so with pious pornography. It often parades as adult entertainment, diversion, advertisement, or sophistication, and that it may be. But the effects are the same. And a Christian must doubly be on guard. Our survey of some of the major problem areas is justified.

MOTION PICTURES AND TELEVISION

The entertainment media has its share of pious pornography as may be gathered from an investigation of various movies and television shows. A number of general release films combine pornography with a measure of artistic merit. What is truly exploitative or offensive is not two people making love on screen, or on stage for that matter; it is the sexual act employed solely as a come-on, without in any way enlarging our understanding of the characters involved or the nature of love. It is a bid for more publicity and a bigger cut of movie fares by directors who have neither the talent nor the imagination to portray passion by less explicit means. A gifted artist, on the other hand, can convey the emotion of love with any degree of intensity by a word, a facial expression, or a touch alone; the lack of insight and skill makes the obvious easier than the implied.

Some movies are blatant offenders in this respect. Movies like *Myra Breckinridge, Beyond the Valley of the Dolls, Bluebeard, The Love Machine, Boxcar Bertha, Pretty Maids All in a Row, A Name For Evil, Impossible Object, Seven Minutes, The Adventurers, The Statue,* and *Heironymus Merkin* may do much more to undermine the public morality than all the triple-X "sexploitation flicks" combined. At least the latter do not parade as serious films which enjoy the backing of major film industries, top stars, booking in first-class theatres, and reviews in the regular newspaper media.

Another type of pornography in movies is the kind of film that misleads the audience through a dishonest, distorted view of things. In the late fifties and early sixties there was a rash of the Doris Day-Rock Hudson genre of films; the audience was entertained with the predictable, stereotyped "will-they-or-won't-they-and-if-so-when" type of epics. During the same period serious "religious epics" were filmed which purported to glamorize the events of the Bible. Rather than telling Bible history the way it really was, films like *The Ten Commandments, King of Kings, Samson and Delilah, David and Bathsheba, The Greatest Story Ever Told,* and *The Bible* primarily proved that biblical extravaganzas could be the portrayers of stereotyped characterization and glamorized sex (even elaborate orgies could be suggested) and violence. Many a church group packed into the old church bus for a cruise to see at group rates special showings of George Stevens' *Greatest Story*, in which blonde, fair-skinned Carroll Baker played a Jewish woman and Swedish actor Max von Sydow played a pale, almost anemic Jesus who floated through a potpourri of gospel sketches spouting scriptures in unctious tones from the Revised Standard Version.[1]

With the exception of productions like *Jesus Christ Superstar* and *Godspell*, which will not be analyzed here, religious films and plays do not seem in vogue now. But mild pornography persists in other types of productions which succeed by stereotyping some person or profession via hackneyed story line and pointless exploitation of sex and violence. Permit two examples.

In the 1970's, the poor medical profession has had a rough siege of it. Scripts portraying medical misdemeanors have merited Oscars, at least on two occasions. I speak of Richard Hooker's *M*A*S*H* and Paddy Chayefsky's *The Hospital*, two generally entertaining and worthwhile productions. Then a better known Otto Preminger gives us a movie entitled *Such Good Friends*, a supremely superficial and senile exposition of the American way of adultery that says nothing much about human nature in the action of the characters, and certainly nothing nice. If the film were taken seriously, which is highly doubtful, one might suspect that all doctors commit adultery with male patients' wives on the sly and that removing a simple mole from the neck is a high-risk operation. And there is a nude scene, supposedly of actress Dyan Cannon; but since she refused to do the scene, and such a hackneyed film "needed" it to attract voyeurs, Miss Cannon appears

---

1. See a review by Fred Myers in *Christian Century*, April 21, 1965. Pier Paolo Pasolini's *The Gospel According to St. Matthew* is a notable exception to the general run of religious epics.

through the "miracle" of pasted-together trick photography.

Progress, in screen terms of racial stereotyping, is not always a forward thing. In the early seventies over fifty films were produced deliberately to appeal to booming black audiences. Instead of reproducing the Stepin Fetchit stereotype of the thirties, audiences are given the "Shaft." The new stereotype is that the black man is some oppressively potent, super-sexed, super-cool dude capable of killing when the occasion calls for it. Movies like *Shaft* and its sequels, *Blacula* (a black rehash of "Dracula hokum"), *The Legend of Nigger Charley*, and *Melinda* got the black ball rolling. Civil rights leader Julius Griffith, founder of CAB (Coalition Against Blaxploitation), stated that such films are "warping . . . our black children's minds with filth, violence and cultural lies," and that this new stereotype "is just another form of cultural genocide."[2] Griffith probably did not overstate the case.

Some films are pornographic, if only in the mildest sense, because they are simply banal and trivial. "In the last episode, you remember, Zira and Cornelius, the egghead chimpanzees who had come back from the year 3000 via a time warp, were hunted down and killed by their human hosts, who were frightened by the prospect of a future world run by apes. In the next installment . . . ." Promotional material for the next children's matinee? Hardly! Many readers may recognize this come-on as one of the most successful movie series since the progeny of Frankenstein. Twentieth Century-Fox's

2. *Nashville Tennessean*, August 31, 1972. The controversy stirred up by the new spate of black movies is discussed in a cover story, "Black Movies: Renaissance or Rip-off," *Newsweek*, October 23, 1972, pp. 74-82.

Planet of the Apes, Beneath the Planet of the Apes, Escape from the Planet of the Apes, and *Conquest of the Planet of the Apes* have already taken in up to $150 million at box offices around the world and created a new, minor cult of "ape addicts." In spite of obvious banality, perhaps the films are justified by their satire of the human condition.

When I was a child, a cat was a lovable pet, a dog was man's best friend, and a rodent was a funny, likeable, big-eared mouse named Mickey. Beginning in 1971 with *Willard,* there has been a vogue in animal horror flicks to give children new and perhaps not so harmless images. *Willard* was the tender and touching story of a boy's unaffected love for his pet rat, which led a revolting pack that devoured him. With *Willard* grossing $8,200,000, we have the sequel rat saga, *Ben,* as well as *Frogs, The Night of the Lepus* (Janet Leigh is eyed by 1500 mad, mutant rabbits), *Dr. Phibes* (bats, bees, rats, and locusts are on angry prowl), and other such films under contract. One wonders whether such films represent a very good investment of a Christian's time and money.

Of course television does not escape the general indictment offered here. A number of shows at least mildly exploit and shock our sensibilities by what is shown or said. Shows like "Love American Style" and "Laugh-in" certainly treat sex, social hypocrisies, and taboos humorously, but are the treatments fair and honest? What will be the effect on our young adolescents who are exposed to line after line of double entendre sex quips on programs like "The Tonight Show" and "The Dean Martin Show"? When the average viewer is bombarded with this kind of material evening after evening, it leads to a "tyranny of sex." By this I mean that if anything can be taken two ways, it is always taken the sexual or dirtier way. And in real life this inadvertently calls up to our mind sexual connotations for words like "nice girl," "good boy," "relations," "wild time," "obscene," whether they were intended that way or not; even "intercourse" used to have a non-sexual meaning.

Commercial television, operating on the principle of giving people what they want, has its lion's share of trivial programming. The line-up of programs often constitutes the "bland leading the bland." "What does your husband like to sleep in on his least romantic evenings?" Or to the husbands, "If three ladybugs competed in a race around the three main measurements of your wife's body, which one would come in last?" This sort of innocuous—and, undoubtedly to some viewers, highly amusing—trivia is standard fare on many programs like "The Newlywed Game."

Traditionally among daytime television's biggest profit makers are the daily soap operas, watched by 35 to 40 million people, mostly women and especially housewives with presumably nothing better to do. The more liberal code now permits more explicit treatment of such topics as murder, rape, insanity, terminal illness, and, of course, adultery. Does this mean a more honest treatment of life? Well, husbands and wives can be shown together in bed—with naked shoulders, no less! Women are more active in the professional world these days and there are even leading black doctors and lawyers happily employed in Sudsville. All well and good! But the main message to viewers is that you're not a normal person without a day by day grappling with some crucial moral crisis. And how could an otherwise healthy and normal woman get through life without encountering at least one extramarital experience? ("I love you, Howard, but I'm carrying Brian's baby," one woman exclaims on the now defunct "Bright Promise.") Illegitimate pregnancies are more of a problem on daytime TV than in real life. Some weeks it seems as if no one is born in wedlock; even then the father is often in doubt. A number of intelligent women share this critique. In the opinion of NOW (National Organization of Women), the largest of the women's liberation organizations, "sexist" serials and quiz shows are neither innocuous nor amusing—and are not limited to daylight hours. After two years of observing television programming, NOW concluded that TV is saturated with programs that demean women and in May, 1972, filed a petition with the Federal Communications Commission charging that "Not one program of any intellectual, educational or informative content was broadcast during the hours reserved for women's viewers."[3]

NEW-STYLED SEX MANUALS

A new kind of pornography has been surfacing in the 1970's, and its widespread proliferation merits Christian concern. I refer to the deluge of mostly paperback editions of sex manuals offering simple, printed instructions for the ideal sex life.

The whole thing did not begin with Dr. David Reuben, really. In cultures that have encouraged adolescents to delay sexual experimentation until after marriage, "love books" have served as aids to newlyweds who are often faced with some fast on-the-job learning.

---

3. *Newsweek*, May 15, 1972, p. 57.

In Japan young newlyweds were given "pillow books"—
so designated because they were kept beneath the pil-
lows of bridal beds—which illustrated with woodcuts the
myriad means of loving. Some fifteen centuries ago, the
Indian writer Vatsyayana composed the "Kama Sutra"
(Kama is the Hindu god of love and Sutra means text), a
work full of ingenious and poetic elaborations of fore-
play and coitus. In more recent times, Americans since
the 1920's have weathered years of euphemistic explica-
tion by the old masters of sex books like Havelock Ellis
(*Studies in the Psychology of Sex*), Theodore Van de
Velde (*Ideal Marriage*), and Dr. Albert Ellis, a New York
psychologist who published the first widely read books
that broke firmly with the tradition of marital romance
and sexual piety.

As though the old masters were not enough we have
been swamped with a plethora of new "sex manuals." I
refer in part to *Everything You Always Wanted to
Know About Sex But Were Afraid to Ask, Any Woman
Can!* or the imported *ABZ of Love*. But the real examples of pornographic rhetoric are works like *The Sensuous Woman* by "J," *The Sensuous Man*, by "M," *The
Couple*, by Mr. and Mrs. K, and their scores of cheap
imitators. These publications are not faulted because
they are as filled with errors and personal biases as were
the old marriage-ecstasy guides.[4] Neither are they
faulted for unequivocal advocacy of premarital and
extramarital experiences. They must be criticized from
the Christian perspective because they present a dishonest view of sex. With all the fancy labels, cute and

---

4. See "Sex: How to Read All About It," cover story of *Newsweek*, August 24, 1970, pp. 38-43.

simple language, and daring analogies, these manuals demean sex while pretending to extol it.

If you doubt that taking these books seriously is a very degrading experience, spend an hour reading *The Sensuous Woman*—a giddy mixture of field hockey exhortation and whorehouse giggles. "J" gives a number of special maneuvers with catchy titles (one is called "Butterfly Flick"), advocates imagining ball bearings in the hips and presents this basic criterion for choosing a bed-partner: "Does he treat your breasts like unripe grapefruits? Who needs him?" Reuben's *Everything*, the most popular sex manual ever published, contains misinformation or unsubstantiated claims ("blind girls particularly become adept at secret masturbation," or "the more potent a man becomes in the bedroom, the more potent he is in business"). But Reubenian style exploits sex with such terms as "Mr. Sperm" and "Orgasm Central."

"If you can get *at* a woman, you have at least a chance of getting *into* her." That about sums up all that *The Sensuous Man* has to offer—another volume that degrades sex under the pretense of offering advice and consent. More appalling, because it is less clearly meretricious, is Harold and Joan K's candid account of a fortnight at the Masters and Johnson clinic on a holy crusade for Harold's potency.

This new genre of pornography is written as much by women as men. A book by Joyce Peterson and Marilyn Mercer, *Adultery for Adults*, aims at explicating the advantages of extramarital enrichment. Horizontal improvement, they insist, "strengthens marriage," "keeps you and your spouse alert and alive," "opens vistas you can share," and is highly beneficial to the family unit

("Happy parents make happy children"), is "a civil right
of women," is "good for general health," "improves
your grooming," and "helps the national economy."
The authors tell how to begin, and proceed to discuss
logistics (where to go and how often), occupational
hazards, dangerous partners, role of third parties, tips
for travelers, cross-cultural adultery, how the injured
party should behave, and how to dissolve the affair. The
world will never be the same! Another "how-to-behave-
in-bed" handbook is Ruth Dickson's *Now That You've
Got Me Here, What Are We Going to Do?* "Talking
mouth to mouth is yummy and very sexy," it claims.
"Don't forget that the lips are home base . . . come back
up every once in a while for a little mouth-to-mouth
resuscitation," coos the author in another typical pas-
sage. Then there's Natalie Gittelson's *The Erotic Life of
the American Wife.* With the passing of "Mrs. Good-
wife" has emerged the phallic, "resexualized" wife, reports Gittelson with a sturdy supply of four-letter
words, sensational title, and fairy-tale happy ending.[5]

A Christian should be opposed to this pornographic
rhetoric for two reasons. First, none of the manuals
redefine anything or present anything more than what
has been presented in earnest loremongering for two
millennia. The only change has been more descriptive
terms and titles of sexual maneuvers in order to sell
more copies. Books that might really change a society's
sexual customs, taboos, and wisdom are works like

---

5. In fairness, not all the new volumes of the seventies are
   exploitative. See Mary Jane Sherfey, M.D., *The Nature and
   Evolution of Female Sexuality* (Random House, 1972), and
   Barbara Seaman, *Free and Female: The Sex Life of the
   Contemporary Woman,* (Coward, McCann and Geoghegan,
   1972) Book reviews in *Newsweek,* July 3, 1972, pp. 71-72.

Alfred Kinsey's pioneer study quantifying what sexual behavior in America actually is, and Masters and Johnson's demonstrations of the physiological nature of orgasm and the clinical cure of many major sexual disabilities.

Second, and more important, the simple fact is that hundreds of thousands of disillusioned unfortunates who lack—or believe they lack—a full experience of sexuality purchase and consume such tawdry masquerades in hopes of becoming better and more valued people. Instead, they become victims of propaganda. The central, underlying message of all these works (and I would include some serious studies, like those of Masters and Johnson) is that sex is an art form and the key to ultimate value and desirability is in sexual prowess. These pioneering researchers have supplied descriptions in meticulous detail of how sexual intercourse is carried out, how much the pulse rate increases, how the body temperature changes, and the muscles tense. The "true believers" now have "chapter and verse" documentation. One writer facetiously suggests that "we can construct from the data the Perfect Sex Act and get it preserved for all time in silver at the National Bureau of Standards," or "the model ought to be exhibited in the Museum of Modern Art."

As sexual athletes, the manuals supply all kinds of exercises and remedies the readers can employ, the sole purpose of which is to keep the sex organs operating at peak efficiency. One big problem is that many manuals tyrannize conscientious readers by imposing a uniform response on everyone, irrespective of differences in age, personality, and life situation. Sexual intercourse is promoted even as a means of dealing with non-sexual problems (such as loneliness, unpopularity, frustration, etc.).

Orgasms must be sought with religious zeal. An orgasm becomes "the inalienable right of every man and woman." The very change of language from "we need to love" to "we need an orgasm" will subconsciously diminish the value of interpersonal relationship and lessen the importance of the particular sex partner—if indeed any sex partner is needed at all! Christians must be continually warned of the ever-present danger of confusing ends and means.[6]

MASS MARKET SEXUALLY ORIENTED PUBLICATIONS

An even more financially productive form of pious pornography is the mass market paperback books and periodicals which are almost totally sexually oriented. Total sales for romantic confession magazines, barber shop magazines, and other sensational magazines and newspapers will run as high as twenty million copies per month.[7] Stories in romantic confession magazines pri-

---

6. Two recommended critiques of the sex manuals are Earl H. Brill, *Sex is Dead* (New York: Seabury, 1967) and Eugene C. Kennedy, *The New Sexuality* (New York: Doubleday and Co., 1972). Relevant portions of the Brill book may be found in his article "Sex is Dead," *Christian Century*, August 3, 1966, pp. 957-59, and excerpts from Kennedy's book may be found in his article "Sex Isn't Everything," *Reader's Digest*, September, 1972, pp. 49-50. A well-known existentialist psychiatrist, Rollo May, in commenting about the new sex clinics, has stated, "while some clinics do free people for a better relationship, many undermine the fact that sex is connected with tenderness. Certainly nothing is wrong with technique as such, in playing golf or acting or making love. But the emphasis beyond a certain point on technique in sex makes for a mechanistic attitude toward lovemaking, and goes along with depersonalization." *Newsweek*, November 27, 1972, p. 72.

7. See *Presidential Commission*, pp. 108-25 for breakdown.

marily emphasize the sexual problems of young women and are aimed at an audience of adolescent girls and young women. Apparently a large number of older women find them enjoyable reading as well. "Barber shop" magazines feature "adventure" stories whose stock in trade is brutal sadistic "action" stories with "glamor" or "pin-up" photographs serving as a secondary feature of the magazines. A large number of detective magazines, exposé journals, and paperback novels aim at the pornological reader. Not as widespread but definitely pornographic are "figure-study" journals which purport to offer nude figures for the aspiring artist to study, "male art" magazines, and psuedo-nudist magazines. No wonder poet e. e. cummings called such lurid literature "uncomic non-books."

This type of pornography, like the other pious forms we have examined, may be more of a threat to Christian morality because they parade as innocent, worthwhile, and enlightened entertainment. They exploit the natural human instincts and curiosities associated with sex for commercial gain. Their come-on is sensationalism. Each magazine strives to outsell the others on the basis of catchy story lines that will attract the drug or grocery shopper. One I saw recently in a supermarket said: "My husband brought me a new sex gadget and said, 'Try it, you'll like it.' " Another: "My doctor told me my inverted nipple looks erotic." Just from an artistic view, it is sad to see sales so high when hacks contrive the same old plots month after month with little variation.

Not that the exploitation of sex is confined to hard- and soft-core pornography. Top quality magazines (like the now defunct *Life* and *Look*) have frequently resorted to running photographs intended as much to keep readers' interest and sales perked up as to maintain sophistication. And once every few months, a news magazine like *Time* or *Newsweek* will give several pages of full color coverage to women's fashions in swim or evening wear.[8] It's doubtful that even vivid, colorful photo coverage of the new automobiles introduced each fall would be half as interesting without the presence of female models. Paperback publishers repeatedly put sex or violence come-on covers on new books or even on reprints of serious literary efforts. Advertising spreads for these books or new movies skillfully employ sexual stimuli as attention-getters.

Another type of pornographic exploitation that has received little attention by moralists is the invasion of privacy of important persons whose every thought and activity is of interest to the general public. The overly curious and leering segment of the general public gets its kicks by reading the latest documentary and/or pictorial exposé of its heroes, leading political figures, and entertainment stars. The sensational headlines and story titles promise more than the report can really deliver ("Is it true that Joan has never slept with Teddie since Chappaquiddick? Answer: No.), but half the fun is in trying to figure out what the titillating headlines really mean. One lampooning magazine pasted together a nude foldout of Henry Kissinger. And in late 1972, the Italian magazine *Playmen* produced a popular number featuring fourteen

---

8. I recommend that the reader see as two examples *Time's* color photo-coverage of "the nude look" in the June 27, 1972 issue, pp. 77-78, and *Newsweek's* cover story and pictures "Throwaway Chic for Fall," August 21, 1972 issue, pp. 48-56. Also see *Newsweek's* color photo coverage of the film *Last Tango* or its cover photo on sex clinics showing two young, beautiful models suggestively unclad. A realistic cover would have shown a balding, pudgy forty-five year-old man with his sagging spouse.

shots in full color of Jacqueline Kennedy Onassis in the nude on her private beach. This kind of exploitation is motivated by unadulterated, unmitigated love of the almighty dollar and cannot be taken lightly by those who want to discover pornography in its many and varied forms.

A SUI GENERIS

Because of its impact on the American scene, one special kind of publication deserves separate treatment. *Playboy* is unique in the entertainment media and is more of an institution than a publication. The history of its incredible success story is by now legend. Hugh Hefner broke his affiliation with *Esquire* and later purchased a nude photo of Marilyn Monroe to run as his first playmate foldout in 1953. The first issue was not dated, as Hefner was not certain that another issue would be financed. Today Hefner heads the most prosperous empire ever built on sex, which has made him a millionaire 120 times over. His magazine reaches seven million readers a month and sets new records for advertising revenue with almost every issue. Other published material includes anthologies, books, calendars, special editions, and a newer, more erotic publication called *Oui*, begun in October, 1972. Playboy clubs and vacation resorts continue to spring up in all areas of the western world. Excepting the little bunny, the major identifying symbol of the Playboy empire is the monthly playmate foldout in the center of each issue; but *Playboy* represents and promotes in all its use of the media a special philosophy, a special life style. Any critique of *Playboy* must take into account this larger context.

Is *Playboy* pornographic? Or is it merely what it

claims, "entertainment for men?" What should be the church's attitude toward this philosophy? Is the magazine appropriate entertainment for Christian men and women? In the final analysis, each person will have to work out these answers for himself. Time will not be taken here to explain in detail all the factors for consideration on this matter. The serious reader will find several theological critiques of the Playboy philosophy. Herbert W. Richardson's *Nun, Witch, Playmate* (Harper and Row, 1972) is a recent, but brief, analysis. An older critique, which has been parroted, even plagiarized, in many a volume and journal since, is Harvey Cox's article in *Christianity and Crisis* (April, 1961) and his best selling *Secular City* (Macmillan, 1965). The entire philosophy is the subject of a volume by William S. Banowsky, *It's a Playboy World* (Revell, 1969), and there are chapters in Richard F. Hettlinger's *Living With Sex: The Student's Dilemma* (Seabury, 1966) and Donald B. Strobe, *Faith Under Fire* (Word Books, 1969). A critic of the literary and screen arts, Pete Michelson, offers a critique in his book, *The Aesthetics of Pornography* (Herder and Herder, 1971). Michelson's major criticism—that "*Playboy's* pornography consists in its transformation of women into Playmates and bunnies, into erotic art objects designed to titillate the sexual sense and then sublimate it into spending money"—parallels the theological critiques.

Playboy magazine and the philosophy that undergirds it has much to commend itself. Every month the magazine brings its readers some of the very finest material in print, packaged in the most thoroughly professional and attractive formats available anywhere in the world. *Playboy* fiction frequently features the best names—Vladimir Nabokov, Graham Greene, Joyce Carol Oates—

though not always with their best works. The monthly in-depth interviews are with subjects worth talking to (the late Saul Alinsky and Martin Luther King, Marshall McLuhan, Arnold Toynbee, Charles Evers, Fidel Castro, Albert Speer, Ralph Nader, Eldridge Cleaver, and Howard Cosell), and the interviewees speak with a candor and openness not to be found in *Reader's Digest* or *U.S. News and World Report.* The Forum carries well-considered opinion. A few fine pieces on religion and morality have appeared. A number of important political, social, and economic issues have been treated in some depth, and the magazine has been ahead of the church on some issues. Some of the jokes and cartoons offer valuable satire on individual and societal hang-ups and double standards. So it is not true that *Playboy* is just another high class "girlie magazine"; there are plenty of imitators that pander to a more prurient interest. One valuable contribution of the Playboy philosophy has been to expose the weaknesses of "moralism" or legalism, defined here as a prepackaged set of rules and regulations which can be applied equally to every situation, absolute and unbending moral laws which are unalterable. *Playboy* has preached that sex is good and that is that. Pleasure *per se* is not sinful and man should seek to enjoy his life on earth. For decades the church has failed to get that message across, probably because Christians haven't believed it. If the church had really been about its task of promoting a healthy view of human sexuality to the world, there would have been little market for *Playboy* pinups.

There are two main arguments against Playboyism. First even though it virtually worships the female form, *Playboy* is largely anti-feminine. The magazine is at least semi-pornographic because it exploits the bodies of young women to sell copies. In fact one older criticism of the female forms shown has been their atypical qualities; the women are predominantly young, unmarried, and in the larger pictures and fold-outs appear glossily unreal, plasticized, and antiseptic. The philosophy proclaims the idea that the ultimate goal in life is having fun. Women play an important role in the pursuit of pleasure but they must stay in their place; their place is exactly where men want them to be.

It may be countered that *Playboy* has more going for it than beautiful, unclad girls. That we have admitted. But remove the nudes and saucy cartoons from the magazine and it is doubtful that it would retain one-fourth of its present sales. L. E. Sissman lambasts the highly commercialized (though not conspiratorial) brainwashing process occuring in our society when our sexual feelings are raised for us by some contact with a book, magazine, or movie. To Sissman, *Playboy* is the proto-villain of all this, "the first mass pusher of the drug of sex to the sensually disadvantaged of all ages, the first mass packager of denatured (and dehumanized) female flesh, the first mass marketer of measured doses of addictive sexual sensation."[9] *Playboy* went about "its dirty work of prettifying, trivializing, and making palatably cute" its Bunnies as paid temptresses, argues Sissman, and the magazine's "central marketing strategy is to sell fantasies of women as powerless, grateful sexual slaves to men who have found women far otherwise—strong, demanding, and frightening in real life."[10]

Methodist Minister Ralph A. Cannon stated the same criticism from a theological perspective:

9. "The Sex Biz," *The Atlantic*, August, 1971, p. 24.
10. *Ibid.*

The magazine still assumes that sex is a plaything with no significance beyond a moment's pleasure. . . . As long as *Playboy* panders to a juvenile fascination with sexual trivia while calling itself sophisticated, it remains a menace to Christian character. . . . It is not primarily the sheer quantity of unadorned flesh and unrefined language in these periodicals that elicits our concern. Rather it is the over-all ideology—the notion that women are playtime toys for men to dawdle with; that sex is merely a biological function, in the same category as eating and breathing, and to be indulged at will; that love is just a sentimental impediment, an unnecessary complication; that erotic pleasure is the supreme good in life. It is this ideology that makes these magazines vile.[11]

The fact that this case against *Playboy* is at least ten years old does not affect its validity. The editors of *Playboy* seem to have been the most up-tight about this criticism and have arranged several opportunities to refute it. The nudes are not pornographic, we are told, because they are tastefully photographed. This may be true to a large extent. But a number of candid photos of movies in the making or pictorial documentaries of sex in cinema which frequently grace the pages more closely resemble the kind of shots that were once sold under the counter than sanitized Playmates.

With twenty years of experience, some new signs are appearing, slowly but surely. Women's letters are pub-

---

11. Ralph A. Cannon, "Pornography, Sex and the Church," *Christian Century*, May 1, 1963, p. 577.

lished, their viewpoints are supported in the forum and the "Playboy Adviser," and their writings are represented. Articles on women's lib and liberalized abortion have appeared. Women are less air-brushed now and more and more liberal amounts of pubic hair crop up—probably more to keep up with the times (and sales) than to present women realistically. Male frontal nudity will probably be appearing in the near future. Playmates are featured as college or career girls with real interests, hobbies, goals, and boyfriends. Regardless of these changes, the underlying tone of the philosophy is the same—pleasure is an end in itself and women exist for the primary purpose of fulfilling man's masturbatory fantasies. The plain fact is that most women's lib leaders are categorically opposed to *Playboy* and what it stands for and this is perhaps the only issue on which conservative Christians and "women libbers" will find themselves aligned on the same side.

A second criticism may be leveled against the Playboy philosophy. *Playboy* advocates a life style that is at odds with Christian ideals. If the life of Christ has relevance today ("Foxes have holes, and the birds of the air have nests; but the Son of man has nowhere to lay his head"[12]), if Christ's dictum to the rich young ruler ("sell what you possess and give to the poor"[13]), if the example of self-denial in order to share with others which characterized the early community of believers— if all of this means anything today, it means that the Christian cannot afford to embrace the life style of the Playboy.

When one peruses the ads and pictorial features, the

---

12. Matthew 8:20.
13. Matthew 19:21.

overall picture is materialism unbounded. The average young man will probably never have the opportunity to purchase, or even rent, a yacht. The "Playboy pads" frequently featured are so highly priced as to be out of reach of all but a very small percentage of people today. With the world becoming more and more over-populated, with our precious resources, including land itself, dwindling away, with less wealth to share and inflation eating away at what we do have, the majority of readers do not have the resources to handle the epicurean life style depicted by *Playboy* or its well rewarded advertisers. Until a young man reaches the pinnacle of financial success, he will be compelled to forego the finest in living accommodations, automobiles imported from Europe, expensive motorcycles, dune-buggies, electronic gadgets, the latest clothing fashions, and the finest foods and liquors. But if he reads *Playboy* he may feel cheated.

This indictment of *Playboy* could, of course, be applied to many other magazines and other forms of media. But *Playboy* seems more richly to deserve it. We refer again to a statement made earlier in another context: we are to love people and use things, not vice versa, even if the persons involved don't object to being "thingified." The warning of the apostle Paul is not to be taken lightly: "Those who want to be rich fall into temptations and snares and many foolish harmful desires which plunge men into ruin and perdition. The love of money is the root of all evil things, and there are some who in reaching for it have wandered from the faith."[14]

So, we ask again, is *Playboy* fit for Christian con-

---

14. I Timothy 6:9-10.

sumption and entertainment? Unlike many moralists, I do not offer a blanket condemnation. An honest and individual appraisal by each potential reader of his age, maturity, and purpose should determine much of this answer.

A word to the church: like it or not, *Playboy* is popular with the youth, both in and outside of organized religion. Hundreds of thousands of America's religious, academic, and political leaders read *Playboy* in order to keep abreast of contemporary thought on modern issues. It is estimated the magazine has a readership greater than the subscription lists of all the scholarly journals combined. There is much the older generation of church members will see and despise in the magazine. But denunciations will be in vain. Unveiling a meaningful alternative to the Playboy life style is the only thing that will work.

We could spend a great deal of time discussing magazines in the Playboy style. In fact, one important indication of *Playboy's* success is the numerous imitators that have moved into the market to compete for revenue. None has made much of a dent in *Playboy's* potential readership, with one exception—a British publication named *Penthouse*, which by January, 1973, had a worldwide monthly sale of nearly 3,000,000. The chief purpose of *Penthouse* seems not to add any new insight to human sexuality but to outsell *Playboy* by showing more but less glossy nudes and more lurid cover shots, and by speaking of sex in a bolder, bawdier manner. One issue contained an absurd article by a physician addressed to the coronary-prone and entitled "Commit Adultery and Live Longer." The same presumably typical issue featured a sexual advice column with Xaviera ("The Happy Hooker") Hollander answering intimate inquiries and a reader discussion of the merits of using enemas for sexual stimulation. The regrettable thing is to see this magazine adorn the counters of many drive-in markets and main line grocery stores.

Before leaving the subject of pious pornography in magazines, one other periodical has earned enough merit for special mention. When Helen Gurley Brown, author of *Sex and the Single Girl* and several sequels, took over the helm of *Cosmopolitan,* her main goal was increasing the magazine's circulation. That she has done by turning the magazine into a *Playboy*-type journal for women. The magazine is an adapted rehash of *Reader's Digest*-type pep stories on good grooming, fashion, and keeping slim and trim; but it goes one step further by accepting, even defending, the "one-night affair." Perhaps the greatest claim to fame was *Cosmo's* running of the first male centerfold—a reclining Burt Reynolds wearing nothing but his toupee and having a strategically placed wrist. In most cities, the special issue sold out within two hours after it hit the newsstands.

SEX AND THE MARKETPLACE

More than a generation ago, Philip Wylie created a sensation when he suggested, in his *Generation of Vipers,* that a central message of much advertising was, "Madam, how good are you in bed?" His comment is even more apropòs today, for, perhaps the most obvious exploitation of human sexuality is in the marketplace. The crass marketing of sexuality has for several years been an earmark of American advertising techniques. The latent message of much current advertising is, "Dear Madam or Sir, purchase our product and it can help you be more sexually with it." Critics have called this to our attention many times but there seems to be little change in promotional policies; in fact, with the sexual revolution in full swing, the ads seem only to get bolder. Never before have Americans been so receptive to sexual connotations in auditory and especially visual stimuli. This takes on more significance when one learns that the typical consumer pays some attention to an average of seventy-six advertisements a day and is exposed to many more subliminally. Today's advertising is an indirect form of sex education because it conveys images of the conduct of men and women. The images we formulate from advertising help to mold our impressions of appropriate dress, grooming, and behavior, and may be far more influential than conventional sex education and family home training. Psychologists believe that the typical child entering his first grade of formal education has already spent more time watching television than he will devote to the classroom rituals of the next six years. And from 10 to 15 per cent of that television time is devoted to advertising. So the problem is a significant one.

What product today is not marketed without the sugar coating of sex? Sex is the powerful motivation packaged to make any product irresistible. Through the mass media everything sexless has been sexualized to reap greater profits—automobiles, detergents, deodorants, tobacco, and clothing. Automobile ads may show a micro-skirted lass sprawling all over the body of the latest model with expressions and sighs as though she were on the body of her lover. Though tastefully done, full nudity is now popular in many ads promoting personal items—from Lady Remingtons, Revlon cosmetics, Landlubber clothes, Esquire socks, Sardo Bath Oil, to Elizabeth Arden bath preparations. An ad for Sony tape players pictures a young bikini-clad lady reclining on the beach with three admiring fellows looking on under the caption "Sony and the single girl." A television ad shows another bikinied miss retrieving a Bic ballpoint pen that has just undergone some rigorous test with a crane.

What happens when there is a surfeit of nudity in ads? *Stern,* West Germany's second largest illustrated weekly, may provide the answer. When one of their clients wanted to place an eye-catching ad some new gimmick was needed. Nudes are so common in German magazines that another one would not get readers to look twice. The solution: an obese (5 ft. 3 in., 161 lbs.) model was hired to crouch on the beach holding an umbrella.[15]

One effect of such advertising is to encourage and provide themes for sexual fantasies. The once popular Maidenform brassieres ad demonstrated that a pure sexual appeal, presented in an atmosphere of fantasy, could be successful. "I dreamed I was a _____ in my Maidenform Bra" series was acceptable because the exhibitionist situations shown were part of a dream and, after all, who can be responsible for his dreams? Another fantasy promoted by advertising is that both single and married young men are always in a state of sexual readiness, alert to leap at every available attractive woman whose sexuality is possible only because she regularly uses the recommended product. Some men fall into a river while others teeter and fall off a high-rise construction project when the slim young lass who drinks Diet Pepsi swings by—the ad informs us these men are doing a "doubletake," thanks to Pepsi.

---

15. This story and picture of the ad may be seen in *Time,* August 7, 1972, p. 29.

In less than a minute, a full drama of "before and after" can unfold. First we see a young man happily courting the girl of his choice under moonlight or on the dance floor. All is well until she gets a whiff of his breath (or armpits, possibly from ventilated armpits), or sees a few too many flakes of dandruff deposited on his shoulders. The romance is on the rocks. Along comes a friend the next day who just happens to have in his pocket the necessary potion. Last scene: the two are together again with the formerly alienated partner holding a bottle of the advertiser's product and volunteering to the viewing audience the secret of his success. Other themes include the imminent collapse of a marriage until the right detergent or laxative is located, or the loss of the pleasures of honeymooning until a bottle of Alka-Seltzer is located.

Much advertising is indictable for the use of sexual imagery or suggestiveness. Promises of sexual fulfillment if a certain brand of after-shave lotion, automobile, razor blade, pair of socks, or even cigars is used are anything but subtle. All television viewers are familiar with the Noxema commercial that zooms in on a wet-lipped voluptuary urging her guy to "take it all off" to the tune of "The Stripper," converting an everyday grooming experience into the excitement of a striptease. Now this product's advertising agency invites us to watch Joe Namath "get creamed." We are informed that one brand of toothpaste gives our mouth "sex appeal." One kind of cologne is called "Skinny Dip." When cigarette ads were on television, there were catchy jingles proclaiming that it's "so round, so firm, so fully packed," or, "it's not how long you make it; it's how you make it long," or "it's what's up front that counts." In Capri we have the first "sexy European" automobile although the criteria for the "sexy" automobile escape most of us. And Datsun has become the "Sensuous Automobile." Clairol's famous "does she or doesn't she?" remains an enormously successful slogan, undoubtedly because of its alternative meanings. A full page color ad for General Electric shows a nude blond cuddling a fur stole to cover strategic areas; the caption above says "Men hate cold women," while to the side we see the ad is for sun and heat lamps. A 1972 ad for Lanvin's "My Sin" shows actress Jennifer O'Neill with a blouse unbuttoned to her waist and spraying her bosom; below are the words "Jennifer O'Neill is a Sinner." Indeed! A subscription advertisement for *Avant-Garde* magazine shows an exotic looking girl standing sexily above the words "A Proposition." Ads for National Airlines have shown attractive, clean-cut stewardesses with this invitation: "I'm Cheryl (or Karen, Laura, Margie, Pat, etc.). Fly me." And on we could go, *ad infinitum.*

If we survive this exhausting bombardment from the media with our values and attitudes intact, is it any wonder we start finding sexual associations even where none were intended? This is just another manifestation of the "tyranny of sex" discussed previously.

Sex in the marketplace also takes another direction. Those old hands at the mating game, the cosmetics manufacturers, refuse to be caught napping by the sexual revolution. Since advertising firms have convinced masses of people that being sexually desirable is the ultimate key to success in business, making friends with folks who count, and landing and keeping a mate, some of these firms are now called upon to create the demand for products heretofore wholly unimagined. Alas, the shelves of once staid drug stores now display rows of scented or flavored douches and genital deodorant sprays for both sexes. But special studies sponsored by *Consumer Reports* discovered that the "feminine hygiene sprays," as they are euphemistically called, not only will not take care of malodors but the consumer runs a risk of burning, inflammation, or other adverse reactions. The journal concludes: "The answer to the immediate problem of genital cosmetics is simple. Don't use them."[16]

CONCLUSION

In conclusion, these seem to be some of the major areas of pornography that are often dismissed because the invasion of privacy, the dishonest view of things, the exploitation of other people, and the distortion of values is so subtly concealed. Too few people are offended by such pious pornography. We had rather exercise our ire over the blantantly offensive, hard-core stuff and are left vulnerable to the effects of the inroads pornography in milder forms makes into our lives and the lives of our children. Whenever the mass media excessively promotes eroticism in whatever form, there is always a potential for negative or detrimental effects upon a person's psyche, not excluding the middle-aged or older person. If sex is universally heralded as the ultimate status symbol, as *Playboy* and the pornocrats preach, many responsible adults may wind up feeling cheated and alienated from the mainstream of "what's happening." It is up to Christians to show the world that love, hope,

---

16. *Consumer Reports*, January, 1972, pp. 39-41. See also "The Sexy Sell," *Newsweek*, April 16, 1973, pp. 87-88, for a report on the new explicitness in clothing and grooming product advertising.

patience, tenderness, courage, and honesty—not sexual prowess—are the qualities that make life really worth living.

QUESTIONS FOR DISCUSSION

1. Do you agree with the author that hard-core materials constitute only a small part of our society's pornography problem?
2. Do you think that R-rated films could be more of a threat to public morality than X-rated films?
3. In what ways have general release films based on Bible stories distorted reality?
4. Marlon Brando turned down his 1973 Oscar for "Best Actor" to protest stereotyping in American films. Do you agree with him that Indians, blacks, and other minority groups have been unfairly stereotyped by the mass media?
5. Is the author expanding the definition of pornography too much when he includes banal and trivial movies and television shows?
6. What is meant by the "tyranny of sex"?
7. Do you think popular writers like Reuben and Masters and Johnson have made great contributions to our society's understanding of human sexual behvior?
8. Do you consider *Playboy* to be a pornographic publication? Does it have any worthwhile features?
9. How does the American mass media teach materialism?
10. Why do you think there is so much sex and suggestiveness in today's advertising? Should anything be done about it?
11. "Commercials are legal pornography!" declares Ti-Grace Atkinson, member of the National Organization of Women and founder of the Feminists. "Women are shown exclusively as sex objects and reproducers, not as whole people." Do you agree?

8

Rethinking Obscenity

Before launching his 1969 evangelistic campaign in New York City, the Reverend Billy Graham took a stroll down 42nd Street, pointing out to a television cameraman lurid pictures in the windows of pornography shops and indicating that these obscenities were proof positive of how far America had strayed from the path of righteousness. The popular evangelist left no doubt that these displays of human flesh were the height of immorality. This kind of "moral decadence," Graham informs us, is "the greatest threat to our democracy."[1]

In January, 1972, the Reverend Mel Perry of Nashville's Grace Presbyterian Church and eight fellow picketers marched in ten degree weather around the Cokesbury bookstore in downtown Nashville. Signs they carried read as follows: "Remember what happened to Sodom and Gomorrah," and "The only sex education we need in the church and in the school is the Bible and the ten commandments." Cokesbury specializes in religious books and supplies so when pressed by reporters as to the obscenity inside, Perry mentioned a calendar with a bare-breasted girl for the April page and "that filthy, dirty book; it has four-letter words all through

---

1. *Time*, July 11, 1969, p. 65.

it." In the case of the latter he was referring to James Baldwin's *Another Country.* [2]

Of course Mr. Perry's extremism is largely outside of the mainstream of Protestantism, or Presbyterianism for that matter. His protest can be dismissed with a chuckle. But the tragic thing is that such a noted and respected spokesman for religion as the Reverend Graham and the many ministers and millions of parishioners who are also of his persuasion have such a limited understanding of what constitutes the obscene.

Thus far in our study the words "pornography" and "sexual obscenity" have been employed synonymously. Previously "obscenity" was defined as offensiveness to the taste, degrading, loathsome, and disgusting. In the great majority of situations, Christians tend to think of the obscene as either sexually oriented materials or so-called dirty words. But if it is true that anything which is offensive to the sense, which dehumanizes and depersonalizes other individuals, or which is abhorrent to morality and virtue are the characteristics of the obscene, then why do Christians get so incensed over sexual obscenity to the virtual neglect of other forms of obscenity? My guess is that we have failed to see anything else but nude bodies as obscene. But Howard Moody points out, in an essay calling for a redefinition of obscenity from a theological focus, that "what is obscene is that material, whether sexual or not, that has as its basic motivation and purpose the degradation, debasement, and dehumanizing of persons."[3]

If Christians would begin thinking of obscenity less in

2. *Nashville Tennessean*, January 16, 1972.
3. Howard Moody, "Toward a New Definition of Obscenity," *Christianity and Crisis*, XXIV (January 25, 1965), 287; the article is highly recommended.

terms of sexual pornography and more in terms of how we think about our fellow man and how we treat him, then we could direct our energies toward eliminating greater obscenity and its effects from our society. In this chapter we will look at the psychology of obscenity and then consider two other forms of obscenity from the Christian perspective—verbal obscenity and violence.

OBSCENITY AND COGNITIVE PROCESSES

True obscenity is accomplished by the objectification and dehumanization of other humans. Its purpose, whether intentional or inadvertent, is the debasement and depreciation of other men and women—their worth and their dignity. Obscenity involves objectification because humans cannot be sold, used to sell, or destroyed so long as they retain in the mind of the buyer, seller, or destroyer their nature as subject. The "peculiar institution" of slavery existed in the South for many years by the decisions of basically "decent" men. How was this possible? Only because people objectified the blacks imported from Africa, considering them something less than full humans, by a refusal to acknowledge their natural and inherent worth as human beings. Blacks living and working in the North during this period lived little if any better; with miserable living conditions and hideous wages they eked out a meager existence. What enables an employer to treat people obscenely and live with his conscience? It is possible whenever a person anesthetizes his conscience to the point that others are sensed as objects or pawns for one to handle or mishandle at will. Stereotyping is a less obvious way of denying that every man is a unique subject (soul/self), but it also enables a person to deal with another obscenely because of the uncomplimentary picture he has in his mind of others in the same group. The act of dehumanization and objectification is not completed overnight. The mental processes that effect it may be weeks, months, and years in development. When these habits of viewing others evolve over a longer period not only are they more ingrained but it is difficult at any one point for the offender to see that he is viewing and dealing with others obscenely. For example, one of history's greatest obscenities occurred in this century. One of the most obscene sights of all time was the herding of naked men, women, and children into giant gas chambers for mass extermination and the shoveling of their bodies into furnaces as though they were lumps of coal placed on a winter fire. But the Nazi conscience that permitted such atrocities did not degenerate overnight. It was preceded by propaganda and lies, scapegoating, discrimination, and persecution. Gradually the latent cruelty of Nazi officials surfaced to the point where Jews were totally stripped of their subjective humanity and dignity and without compunction were treated worse than animals. Of course we are appalled and it would seem incredible that anyone would allow such a policy to be repeated in the future. But we need to be reminded that the same habits of thought are operative among us today.

SECOND THOUGHTS ON VERBAL OBSCENITY

Throughout the centuries, few teachings of the Bible are taken more seriously by those who would live righteously than the dictate that our speech be purged of profanity and blasphemy. Whether or not they have lived up to this requirement of godly living in an exemplary manner, Christians concede that their choice of language is to be different from the worldly-minded. The adrenalin of many a righteous soul has pumped furiously at the sound of four-letter expletives or at hearing the name of God taken in vain. Many a child's mouth has been washed with soap for having accidentally uttered a word or phrase that "no decent person would have thought of."

Is pure language less a virtue today than in 1960 when Republican Presidential candidate Nixon censured former President Harry Truman for his profanity?[4] Perhaps so! Not only does verbal obscenity persist—it has, in fact, become a principal rhetorical strategy of various activist groups. The speeches by spokesmen of the youthful New Left are sprinkled liberally with obscene words and expressions. The comments of Black Power advocates are replete with obscenity. The mobs of antiwar protesters unload shouts of obscenity on politicians running for the high office of the Presidency. Traditional profanity abounds in most movies except those rated "G" and is becoming more and more commonplace in evening television shows. Even John Wayne is much more expressive these days.

Despite the moral indignation it evokes in the minds of most conservative Christians, the new frequency with which it is employed demands another analysis of the whole issue from a Christian perspective.

In order to understand what is real obscenity in speech, a little understanding of semantics is essential. Semantics is the study of meaning, how words and other symbols come to be associated with certain meanings.

---

4. See Theodore H. White, *The Making of the President 1960* (New York: Pocket Books, Inc., 1961), p. 358.

The basic tenet of semantics is that human beings are uniquely free to manufacture, manipulate, and assign values to symbols as they please. To a semanticist, meaning is not in a word or symbol, not in messages, and not in dictionaries. Meanings are in people as covert responses; meanings are learned and they are personal property. To the extent that people share similar meanings, they can communicate. And there is no necessary connection between a linguistic symbol and the idea, emotion, or object it represents. Using Hayakawa's popular analogy, "the symbol is NOT the thing symbolized; the word is NOT the thing; the map is NOT the territory it stands for."[5] Communication effectiveness is limited by people who believe that everyone attaches the same meaning to a word or phrase that they do. Variations in connotative meaning probably accounts for a great portion of the so-called "communication gaps" that exist in our modern society.

The practical application of this theory is that no word, expression, or gesture is obscene *in and of itself.* Obscenity is a function of context. The purpose for which the obscenity is used, who uses it, where it is used, and how it is employed all converge to make communication either obscene or acceptable.

For the Christian, real obscenity should be the kind of language choices that reveal a lower view of some other man or woman, strip him of his dignity, and deny him his unique value. The words of degradation and contempt are not only received as such by the listeners— *they are thus intended!* If an audience perceives a term as connoting disrespect and the speaker intends it con-

---

5. S. I. Hayakawa, *Language in Thought and Action* (rev. ed; New York: Harcourt, Brace & World, 1949), p. 31.

temptuously, true obscenity has been uttered. The real sin is not in the acoustical sounds that have been channeled through sound waves or any concomitant gestures channeled through air waves; neither can profanity or obscenity be inherent qualities of a group of marks, lines, or scratches published on a sheet of paper. The real sin is in the heart of the speaker. The uttered contempt confirms the sin and goes a step further to injure and/or harden the person described and any disinterested third party.

I believe this position on obscenity is biblically sound. The warning of Jesus about an "unpardonable sin," which, he said, was "blasphemy against the Holy Spirit,"[6] can hardly mean that the blasphemy resides in the words that are uttered. The real blasphemy is in a man's total rejection of God's Spirit in his heart and life. Words are symbols that merely confirm that blasphemy. The same principle has been applied here. The essential profanity against God is man's dogged refusal to take Him seriously. The truly profane or obscene word is the one used to deny and denigrate the dignity and humanity of another person as an equal partner of the creation.

If one accepts this premise, it follows that many of the four-letter words that raise pious eyebrows in public are not obscene at all. I refer to terms of urination, excretion, and intercourse one finds copiously etched on public restroom walls. In middle or upper class society the words are generally avoided because at best they are dull, uninteresting, and unimaginative. A Christian avoids them further because, at worst, such words are distasteful, coarse, and vulgar (common). The Chris-

---

6. Cf. Matthew 12:31-37 and Mark 3:22-30.

tian's negative response to these words is not really a religious act, but is basically a class and cultural response which relates to aesthetics and social manners. Do we really believe that four-letter vulgarities are tantamount to an affront to God and the human creation? "Not everyone who says words like 'Lord, Lord,' " even spoken with great reverence and piety, " 'does the truth' of those words," states Moody; "conversely many people who speak roughly in the raw language of vulgarity live in awe of and respect for the mystery of humanity. . . . When a person speaks in raw language he may be trying to say something that nice and prosaic words will not communicate."[7]

Words that fit this new criterion for obscenity are words like "coon," "kook," "honky," "whitey," "dago," "jap," "pollack," "kike," "pig," and "wop" because many people may regard these terms as contemptuous or disparaging of themselves or others.

I suppose the best example of a truly obscene word is one that has been used on numerous occasions by pious and proper church members whose lips and tongue never articulate a four-letter word. The word "nigger" has been hurled contemptuously and offensively at many a black brother with no thought of its degrading and dehumanizing qualities.[8] Some Christians are horri-

---

7. Moody, *op. cit.*, p. 286.
8. No matter how much the term is detested by right-thinking people, it must and does enjoy legal protection even when used in any form of the mass media. When Atlanta lawyer and self-avowed racist J. B. Stoner used the word in his political advertising, the government defended him. The FCC panel stated: "However abhorrent some speech might be to the commission," the FCC must protect the right of free speech for everyone. *Newsweek*, August 14, 1972, p. 47. Because the number of air waves is limited, the government must guarantee equal time for all candidates. See Head, *Broadcasting in*

fied at jokes with a sexual connotation and are able to maintain a piously straight face; but minutes later may repeat a joke that is totally divested of any respect or dignity for a person of a different race, nationality, or creed. "Whatever poisons our minds against human beings, dishonors them as persons, or cuts off communication with them is obscene."[9]

TELLING IT LIKE IT ISN'T

There is another sense in which language can be employed obscenely. When words and euphemistic platitudes are used to *conceal* rather than *reveal* the truth, we have a prostitution of language. There is no use in denying that some politicians have used "states' rights" and "law and order" as masks for injustice to blacks and protesters. "National security" has been employed as an emotional cover-all for the overkill in strategic weapons and, quite possibly, high level governmental corruption.

By his language habits a person can move deeper into insensitivity, indifference, and outright apathy to the needs of others. The term "senior citizen," for example, may rob the elderly of much of the dignity of aging that belongs to them; in addition, the term may do little to enhance our sense of responsibility regarding their wants

America, p. 437. For an excellent in-depth discussion of the moral issues that grow out of the operation of the mass media, see William L. Rivers and Wilbur Schramm, *Responsibility in Mass Communication* (New York: Harper and Row, 1969).

9. Haseldon, *Morality and the Mass Media* p. 115. Bobby Seale once explained his penchant for four-letter words with the terse comment that "the filthiest word I know is 'kill' and this is what other men have done to Negroes for years." Quoted by Mary Ellen Leary, "The Uproar Over Cleaver," *New Republic*, November 30, 1968, p. 23.

and needs. It is easier to be indifferent about our responsibilities to the poor and hungry when we can dismiss them from our minds as simply "underprivileged." It is easier to forget about people trying to survive in disgracefully dilapidated apartment buildings when we describe their living conditions as "substandard housing" rather than slums. A 1965 Jules Feiffer cartoon tells the story of a derelict who is informed he is no longer "poor," he is "needy," then he is "deprived," then "underprivileged," later "disadvantaged," and so forth. After much circumlocution, the man quipped, "I still don't have a dime but I have a great vocabulary."

Much startling truth about modern warfare, the most tragic and most burdensome of social diseases, is concealed behind euphemisms and jargon.[10] In fact, perhaps we should use the word "crusade" instead of "war," since it has been applied by some important person to virtually every major conflict. Related to the conduct of modern warfare is such terminology as "selective service," "task force," "Operation something-or-other" (popular in World War II), "liberation," "sororization," "fraternization," "brainwashing," "police action," "military advisers," and "Defense Department" (formerly the "Department of War"), all of which have been to some extent concocted for a special connotation and are worthy of rhetorical analysis.[11]

10. Anthony Lewis develops this idea in some detail in a column released by the New York Times Service, published in the Nashville Tennessean and other papers, January 5, 1971. Columnist Lewis cites a statement by Jean-Paul Sartre to the effect that "evil is a product of man's ability to make abstract that which is concrete." Lewis adds, "The Vietnam War has shown us how profound an insight that is, and how terrifying in a technological age."
11. The renowned linguist Mario Pei examines the origin and use of some of these terms in "The Voice of Annihilation" in

The rhetoric and propaganda that accompanied all modern wars is filled with examples of euphemistic language manufactured and manipulated to effect public support. The recent "undeclared war" in Vietnam continues to provide examples potent enough for purposes of illustration. We have become much more enraged when a plane was shot down over enemy territory if the aircraft is called a "reconnaissance plane" instead of a spy plane and, of course, a spy ship seems more offensive than an "intelligence ship." The systematic destruction of crops and forests, depriving 600,000 people of their normal supplies of rice and other food, can be accepted as commonplace and all in the line of duty when called a "defoliation program." Mass murder and destruction can be called "pacification" or "peacekeeping action," and "free-fire zones" refer innocently enough to the mass expulsion of natives from their humble villages so an army can kill without compunction every living creature that remains. Who is labeled the "aggressor" and who is labeled the "defender" may depend on which side you are on. What is glorified as a "commando raid" when executed by the "good guys" becomes a vicious "sneak attack" or terrorism when committed by the enemy forces. And is it consistent, critics have queried, for an administration that rightly deplores violence on American campuses to drop tons of bombs on North Vietnam and neighboring Laos and Cambodia and call such action merely "protective reaction strikes?"

William Stringfellow, a well-known ethicist and theologian, believes the corruption of language is "the spe-

---

Words in Sheep's Clothing (New York: Hawthorn Books, Inc., 1969), pp. 111-121.

cies of violence most militant in the present American circumstances." He declares:

> That violence is babel: the inversion of language, verbal inflation, defamation, euphemism and coded phrases, rhetorical wantonness, redundancy, such profusion in speech and sound that comprehension is impaired, jargon, noise, nonsense, incoherence, hyperbole, libel, rumor, a chaos of voices and tongues, falsehood.[12]

Stringfellow acknowledges that this babel incites violence, as the American experience with racism for almost four centuries documents, but he further argues that this babel *is* violence.

Who can doubt that our attitudes and ideas about war are affected by the language we hear used to discuss it and the language we ourselves use in discussing and thinking of it? An uncritical acceptance of the connotation of many modern euphemisms can only enhance the remoteness of war from our everyday affairs and insulate the public conscience against the atrocious consequences of modern conflict.

And while discussing a kind of "pornographic" exploitation of language, I feel impelled to comment on the nature of political rhetoric, especially campaign rhetoric. The Presidential campaign of 1972 saw two men vying for the nation's highest office and each one (or one of his surrogates) engaging in some degree of verbal "overkill." From Senator George McGovern we heard phrases like "the most corrupt regime in American history," and analogies that compared President Nixon

---

12. William Stringfellow, "Must the Stones Cry Out?" *Christianity and Crisis*, XXXII (October 30, 1972), 235.

with Adolph Hitler. Could not McGovern have tempered his language with a qualification such as "Absolute judgments are difficult to offer, but I believe. . . ," or "We know that no man is perfect and there is room for honest mistakes, but. . . ."?

The Nixon camp was hardly guiltless. Vice President Spiro Agnew exclaimed: "McGovern is a politician of the utmost expediency. You can't believe what he says. . . .he is one of the greatest frauds ever to be considered a presidential candidate by a major American party." Secretary of Defense Melvin Laird asserted: "McGovern's proposed defense budget is tantamount to a white flag of surrender. . . .He is the spokesman for the enemy."[13]

Political exposition these days seems to rely more and more on the calculated and skillful use of imprecise language. One of the more popular tools of the trade is the overgeneralization, the indiscriminate use of words and labels whose meaning is almost totally supplied by the subjective responses of listeners. Phrases like "concern," "historic," "vital interests," "patriotic," "radical," "freedom," "justice," "America's finest hour," "peace with honor," and "self-determination" are typical examples. Politicians pursuing an unpopular cause or policy are afraid of a phrase or image that is too specific or vivid (such as Curtis Lemay's suggestion about bombing North Vietnam "back to the Stone Age"). It is indeed a sad day when, in the words of poet Peter Klappert, "we *want* a politician to be honest, but we do

---

13. Both quotes were published in the *Nashville Tennessean*, December 5, 1972, and are typical examples. For many other quotations by both sides in the same vein, see *Newsweek*, October 16, 1972, p. 17, and "Sweet and Sour Political Rhetoric," *Time*, October 16, 1972, p. 18.

not expect him to be," and "a 'good' politician is a 'successful' politician and success in politics seems to depend increasingly on the ability to deceive."[14] One might feel that I am expanding the concepts of pornography and obscenity a bit far with this discussion. Perhaps so. But I want to make clear that human language as well as people can be debased and exploited for selfish purposes. What we must demand is more honesty, both in motives and manner of communication, from the men and women who purport to represent us.[15] And we must remember that one of the problems an intelligent and responsible citizen inherits in judging the weight of dirty words and ideas is that the pornography of violence, of political teasing, and outright political lying is hardly brought before juries. Being aware of the problem may be half of the solution.

OBSCENITY AND PROTEST

Minority groups, seeking to advance their cause, often lace their protests with obscenities. But what possible good can they accomplish by injecting offensive words into a debate or discussion? Does not the use of obscenity only tend to alienate neutrals from their cause? Without attempting in any way to justify the use of verbal obscenity, I believe Christians should be aware of its principal purposes as used by youthful or minority demonstrators in public protest.[16]

---

14. Peter Klappert, "Let Them Eat Wonderbread," *Saturday Review*, October 14, 1972, p. 48.
15. See Perry C. Cotham, "What Ever Happened to Righteous Indignation?" *Mission*, January, 1973, pp. 22-26.
16. I wish to acknowledge my dependence on a very helpful source on this topic. J. Dan Rothwell, "Verbal Obscenity: Time for Second Thoughts," *Western Speech*, XXXV (Fall, 1971), 231-42. The listing of purposes comes from Rothwell.

Verbal obscenity serves its users in five ways:

(1) Even though a substantial portion of the "great Silent Majority" probably has little aversion to private profanity, most people find obscenity unacceptable, even repulsive, on the public forum. So its use serves to create attention. It is a jolting, evocative stimulus to a more traditionally-oriented audience.

(2) Obscenity is employed to discredit the "Establishment" or some majority stand on an issue. It expresses a profound contempt for majoritarian ethics, authority, and values. It communicates the depth of outrage.

(3) Verbal obscenity is used to provoke violent confrontations. This was certainly true at the 1968 Chicago Democratic Convention and in the 1970 Kent State affair, two celebrated cases among scores of others. Undoubtedly youthful agitators hoped to win sympathy for their cause by evoking police over-reaction.

(4) Obscenity serves to express strong interpersonal identification with some in-group or subculture. It is a badge of belonging, a sign that one deserves peer respect.

(5) Obscenity may provide the user with catharsis. If deep-seated hostility and hatred is felt toward another, uttering a term of degradation and abuse with fervor and gusto may be a form of emotional release that eases some tension.[17]

---

17. An excellent statement about the impact of verbal obscenity comes from *New York Times* editor A.M. Rosenthal: "Not much of a discourse takes place when one participant smashes another in the face. And the techniques of present-day militancy often simply are verbal blows in the face. Obscene epithets are blows in the face, and in political struggle they have a deliberate, thought-out function. To look at a man and speak to him vilely is to throw filth in his face. Fascists of the

No matter how "right" or "just" a cause may be, a Christian cannot justify extensive use of profanity and obscenity to accomplish his objectives. That's a rather safe conclusion. But how should a Christian react to verbal obscenity as a rhetorical strategy in the media? Neither suppression nor denunciation of its use is an adequate response. What must be done is to open the lines of genuine communication to those who feel oppressed and abused, to reassure them by our actions that we identify with their plight, and that differences can be resolved by discussion and debate and not on some battlefield of confrontation.

EXPLICIT VIOLENCE AS OBSCENITY

Just as the traditionally "dirty words" are not the basis for verbal obscenity, in the same manner we do not do justice to the biblical theology of sin and immorality if we see sex as the dominant and determinative criterion in the labeling of what is obscene. The whole of Christian doctrine and tradition must be brought to bear on the question.

Though critics have often spoken of sex and violence together—as two regrettable qualities in contemporary movies and television programming, for example—in actual practice we tolerate blood, brain, and guts in a volume and concreteness still denied to the treatment of sexuality. This is a sad irony, since, to my way of

---

right and of the left know that when a man is so addressed he is humiliated and brought down and they know that when filth is thrown the recipient, however decent, suddenly stands amidst the reek. Obscenity is simply one more weapon in political street warfare, and so is racism." *The New York Times,* January 6, 1969, p. 143.

thinking, violence (a negative life force) is an eminently stronger base for censorship than sex (a positive life force, albeit often shot through with human sin and distortion).

When the James Bond-007 features were popular in the mid-sixties, it was fashionable for church critics to worry about the effect explicit sex would have on the morality of young teens who flocked to that genre of film; but it is also curious that many of these same people ignored or dismissed any deleterious effect the display of fancy weapons and Bond's license to kill might have on that same youthful audience. The rising rate of violent crime, and the assassinations of President John Kennedy, Martin Luther King, Jr., and Robert Kennedy caused us to raise new questions about the decency of our nation and the direction in which we are heading. If we are honest with ourselves, we will have to concur with an indictment made by Eric Larabee in 1960: "The true obscenities of American life lie in our vicious public consumption of human suffering, in virtually every form and medium. By comparison, the literature of sexual love would seem vastly to be preferred."[18]

The question of violence in the media opens to us a whole new area that cannot be investigated here. And even if this were our subject, conclusive studies are yet to be completed. One thing is certain—there is an obscenity of violence in the mass media today, the depth of which is so great that the effects upon our citizens cannot be neutral. Christians need to ask what kind of

---

18. Eric Larabee, "Pornography Is Not Enough," *Harper's*, November, 1960, p. 96.

message is being communicated in the entertainment field.

For regular moviegoers the extent and nature of violence needs no lengthy elaboration. The early seventies saw a spate of films featuring ultraviolence, to borrow a term from the stylish sadists in *A Clockwork Orange.* Movie producers found ultraviolence to be ultraprofitable at the box office, the mass audiences found it ultraenjoyable, and enough able critics found this type of film ultraartistic and relevant.

In the highly praised film just mentioned, roving bands of dehumanized hoods deal out a cool, emotionless violence that includes kicking, stomping, gang rape, and beating a woman's brains out with a big phallic sculpture, all the while singing "Singin' in the Rain." Harmless diversion or useful catharsis? Who knows? But the fact that George Wallace's attempted assassin Arthur Bremer saw the film and admitted he "thought about getting Wallace all through the picture. Fantasing myself as the Alek but without 'my brothers.' Just 'a little of the old ultraviolence,' " should be interesting evidence for some kind of theory.[19]

In 1971's "Best Picture," *The French Connection*, Santa Claus tries to crush a fallen kid's rib cage. 1972's "Best Picture," *The Godfather*, shocked audiences of millions with several scenes of vivid executions. In another highly acclaimed film, *Straw Dogs*, producer Sam Peckinpah flawlessly expressed his primitive vision of experience—his belief that manhood requires rites of violence, that home and hearth are inviolate and must

19. See *Newsweek*, August 14, 1972, pp. 22-23. *Time*, August 14, 1972, pp. 22-23.

be defended with bloodshed, and that a man must violently conquer other men to prove his courage and hold on to his woman. Roman Polanski's *Macbeth* dispatches its victims with a vividly slit throat, a broadax in the back, a dagger in the forehead, and a sword in the groin, all only a prelude to decapitation. For the younger set, in *The Cowboys* John Wayne is slowly shot to death by rustlers, then avenged when a group of children torture one rustler and kill them all. Policeman *Dirty Harry* was just that. *The Culpepper Cattle Co.* is another "thoughtfully violent" western and *Prime Cut* was more indiscriminate about sloshing blood around, using it merely as ornamentation for an *Argosy* magazine-caliber gangster story.

Not that violence in movies is a product of the seventies. *Psycho*, the aforementioned James Bond films, *The Wild Bunch*, and *Midnight Cowboy* were only a few of many predecessors.[20] And with *Bonnie and Clyde* new techniques of filming violence were utilized. In an excellent article on "The New Violence," *Newsweek* critic Joseph Morgenstern comments on these techniques:

> Their techniques—slow motion, surreal performances, elegant decor, brilliant editing, fish-eye lenses, repeat frames—seem to comment on the action without saying anything. They lend distance, but they also dehumanize victims in the way that high-fashion photography dehumanizes models, and they create a high-fashion horror that can turn an audience on higher than the real thing. The Vietnamese

---

20. See a special issue of *Esquire* on violence in movies of the middle sixties. July, 1967, pp. 39ff.

war could look lovely in slow motion—Sky-
raiders floating in for the kill like seagulls,
fragmentation bombs opening like anemones.
But the horror would still be horror, with
nothing added by technique.[21]

What is seen in the movie houses today will be tomorrow's "Saturday night at the movies" on television. And
that brings us to the question of the television medium
and violence. Between the ages of five and fourteen, our
children, it is estimated, will witness the annihilation of
12,000 human beings.[22] Violence is the best formula
for holding families together between commercials as a
few hours of "Gunsmoke," "Mannix," "Cade's County," "Hawaii Five-O," "Mod Squad," and "Mission:
Impossible" will confirm. And some of the new movies
made especially for television are more violent if less
realistic than their counterparts showing in town or at
drive-ins.[23]

---

21. *Newsweek*, February 14, 1972, p. 68.
22. Eliot A. Daley, "Is TV Brutalizing Your Child?" *Look*, December 2, 1969, p. 99.
23. In a paper prepared for the Media Task Force entered in "A
Report to the National Commission on the Causes and Prevention of Violence," Monica D. Blumenthal comments on
the mass media's stereotype of heroes and villains. As for
heroes, "they are seldom portrayed as having any capacity for
tenderness or love. They clearly and easily are identified as
being in the 'right.' Never are these one-dimensional characters drawn in such a way as to portray the frailties of human
existence that encumber us all. . . Rarely are villains presented
as people who might love their wives and children, be victims
of circumstance, or nature's accidents. On the vast majority
of occasions, villains are drawn as unidimensional characters
representing a generalized personification of evil who deserve
whatever unpleasant fate lies in store for them. Moreover, not
only are these stories presented with a complete absence of all
the ambiguities and complexities that make it so difficult to
distinguish the good guys from the bad guys in real life, there
is in most presentations the covert message that as long as a

Most behavioral scientists believe that aggressive behavior is learned, often by observation, and some are convinced this violence on television plays a significant role in fostering violent behavior in both children and adults. These convictions now have basis in fact according to studies reported to the Surgeon General in *Television and Growing Up: The Impact of Televised Violence*. The italicized conclusion of this report asserted "that the present entertainment offerings of the television medium may be contributing, in some measure, to the aggressive behavior of many normal children. Such an effect has now been shown in a wide variety of situations."[24]

The significance for Christians should be clear. Each civilization potentially is only two decades from barbarism. Every generation has but twenty years to civilize the children born into its midst. Currently, American youth get more of their education from television than from school and church combined. Is our society paying a high price for the free entertainment, tawdry and vulgar, with its unrelenting themes of murder and mayhem, that is channeled into our living rooms and dens? With the better techniques and more professional film-making, are we deceived by the fact that many films in

---

person is a bad guy, it does not matter what you do to him. In the pursuit of the good cause, any method of bringing the devil to bay is justified; so the marshall shoots the rustler, the policeman beats the murderer, the posse lynches the outlaw, and the secret service agent assassinates the spy. The ethical problems related to the idea that one human being is beating, maiming, killing another human being are never discussed. In fact, the idea that the criminal, spy, outlaw, enemy soldier, etc. is a human being is rarely presented." David L. Lange, Robert K. Baker, and Sandra J. Ball, *Mass Media and Violence* Vol. XI (Washington D. C.: U.S. Government Printing Office, 1969), pp. 490-91.
24. Reported in *Newsweek*, February 14, 1972, p. 66.

question are nothing more than what were a few years ago called "exploitation" films and that there can be a "pornography of violence" more deadly than a pornography of sex? Does an easy empathy with cinema slayings, together with a growing tolerance of real life brutality suggest that, beneath the surface, Americans are less alarmed by murder and sadism—and more attracted to it—then we care to admit? Christian spokesmen should strive to learn and articulate the answers to these questions. Acknowledging an unhealthy fascination with violence should be the first step in coming to grips with it.

REAL LIFE OBSCENITY

Not all obscene pictures are contrived by a writer and director and executed by stunt men on a movie lot in full view of sound cameras and packaged for commercial viewing in Hometown, U.S.A. On the contrary, the most obscene sights in the world are real events and conditions captured by photographers for posterity.

Since my college days I have subscribed to several news and feature magazines on a regular basis. To my knowledge I have never thrown away a single issue as a crowded attic will attest. In getting ready for this study I rummaged at random through some of the old stacks and cut out some truly obscene pictures. Some of these photographs are sickening. If Billy Graham saw anything worse on 42nd Street, I do not know how he could stomach it. Indulge my sharing of these through the printed medium.

There are several pictures of hunger and poverty. One picture is of a young black Biafran mother holding up an uncooked, puny chicken or other bird with starving children surrounding her probably asking for a bite. The woman is topless but if anyone sees anything erotic about the picture he is sick.[25] Another set of pictures shows malnutrition and stark poverty in Appalachia.[26] One picture shows a bull that has been used for fighting and then sacrificed and being dragged by a chain from the arena.[27] There are several color pictures on the slaughter of seals to gratify the greed of man.[28] The characters in Fellini's *Satyricon* are nothing if not obscene.[29]

Photographed victims of personal violence are no less obscene. There is a sickening picture of a young victim of child-beating,[30] and a closeup shot of Elizabeth Hyland, a Roman Catholic schoolgirl, lying in a hospital bed with two huge black eyes, swollen face, and butchered hair; she was the victim of an IRA tar and feathering.[31] No less obscene is the unleashing of police dogs and fire hoses on black demonstrators in Birmingham.[32] A Buddhist monk protesting by self-immolation is hardly a pretty sight.

Photocoverage of war produces the most dehumanizing and degrading views of man that no amount of nudity can match. A feature story entitled "Hiroshima" can almost turn a hawk into a dove. As the magazine says with close-up shots of the victims' faces: "What

25. *Look*, April 1, 1969, p. 25.
26. *Look*, March 4, 1969, pp. 25-26.
27. *Look*, September 3, 1968, pp. 34-35.
28. *Life*, March 21, 1969, pp. 61-63.
29. See *Look*, March 10, 1970, pp. 51-52.
30. *Newsweek*, July 24, 1972, p. 66.
31. UPI telephoto appearing in *Nashville Tennessean*, May 12, 1972.
32. See a special publication of pictures and text covering the civil rights movement, *You Can't Kill the Dream* (Richmond, Virginia: John Knox Press, 1968).

happened on August 6, 1945, is best told not in chronicles but in the remembering eyes and tightening scars of those who emerged from the furnace."[33]

The Vietnamese War produced its share of atrocities. As in all wars, the perpetrators of such violence can only act obscenely when they objectify or deny the essential personhood of their victims. The enemy may actually be a human but only in a peripheral way. And to make certain one continues to think of him that way, the enemy should be called "gooks." The fact that these people are racially distinguishable from us makes a policy of saturation bombing more acceptable. After all, it's not American boys that are dying. But thanks to the media we can know that *both* sides are treating the other obscenely.

In one of the most shocking sights, a Vietcong is carrying in each hand a severed head of the enemy.[34] One picture that received considerable media publicity shows South Vietnam's General Nguyen Ngoc Loan executing at point-blank range a newly captured prisoner suspected of being a Vietcong officer.[35] Another picture shows a Vietnamese (North or South? Does it really matter?) mother with a small child. Both are nude. And both are bombing victims with ugly disfigurations and scars on the child's face and woman's body.[36] Another nude woman is shown backside on a hospital bed. we are told her miserable condition stems from her

---

33. *Look*, August 11, 1970, pp. 38-45.
34. I have had trouble locating this particular picture in my files but I recommend the reader see "A Gallery of Photos that Brought the War Home," *Time*, November 6, 1972, pp. 20-21.
35. *Look*, June 25, 1968, p. 18.
36. *Commonweal*, January 12, 1968, p. 441.

being "on the receiving end of a Honeywell anti-personnel device."[37]

But absolutely the most obscene pictures I have seen connected with this war were published in connection with an open letter to the President by Army neurosurgeon Murray H. Helfant. Seven victims were shown. One fellow, whose injury was described as "fairly typical," had lost his maxillary sinus, both eyes, and both frontal parts of the brain. Another is shown with a pentrating wound to the brain. Another soldier is shown with a leg amputated and still another with his head sewn up like a baseball (literally).[38] Getting away from human subjects, there are pictures of stands of mangroves destroyed by herbicide ("Remember, only we can prevent forests") and another showing dozens of bomb craters disfiguring a Vietnamese farm.[39] Getting away from the war, environmentalists might want to take a look at *Psychology Today's* winning entries in the "Dirty Pictures" contest published in the November 1970, issue.

THE RISK CHRISTIANS ASSUME

These examples chosen among many should suffice. What shall we say about all of this? Should these actual obscenities be censored from our eyes? What are the implications for the teaching and preaching ministry of the church?

First of all, the Christian must assume a risk. He should not for a moment permit the real obscenities of

---

37. Back page, *Christianity and Crisis*, May 1, 1972. See similar pictures in *Life*, June 23, 1972.
38. *Look*, July 28, 1970, pp. 48-53.
39. *Newsweek*, August 7, 1972, pp. 24-25.

life to be removed from his view. Nor should he want those pictures denied to the general public. They show us the cost of war or class strife or racial injustice or religious bigotry. Sometimes this class of obscene pictures is necessary to penetrate solidified minds and hardened hearts. The obscene may rouse people from their apathy and spark new involvement. Further, its use should not be denied the legitimate filmmaker or playwright.

While obscenity may be creative, the risk is that is may be destructive. By permitting ourselves and our children to see such obscenity depicted, we run the risk of coming to accept war, and the myriad forms of injustice that permeate the human society as a natural and realistic way of resolving conflicts between men and nations. Deprivation and degradation are taken in stride. As month after month of evening newscasts churn out the horrors of war and conflict around the globe, the only way we can possibly tolerate it is by turning off the TV or turning off a part of our conscience. This is the risk. But the alternative is no less welcome—a mental straitjacket, closed thought processes, and a third-class society.

Second, there is an important lesson many Christians need to learn. The depths of decadence of a nation or society cannot be measured by such a short measuring rod as sexual explicitness. The popular prophets of folk religion often represent a brand of religion that many Americans feel comfortable with. They speak to crusade and television audiences composed largely of churchgoers. This being the case, listeners enjoy hearing the prophet lash out at our nation's lack of "spirituality," for spirituality is just what they have plenty of. But what about racial injustice in all parts of the country, what about war and poverty and oppression and over-population, etc.? Vague, abstract terms may be called up for a blanket coverage of these terms in passing. What the people come to hear is a crusader "waxing eloquent" on drunkenness, mini-skirts, and naked pictures.

This kind of ministry epitomizes the shame of American religion that talks a lot about little sins and says little about the big sins—that strains at the gnat of sexuality and swallows the camel of dehumanization and destruction. It's a religion that demands personal righteousness but soft-pedals any obligation for social righteousness. It puts emphasis on "spiritual hunger" but ignores physical hunger; it urges "getting right with God" but fails to stress its impossibility without getting right with one's brother; and it keeps before our mind the judgment scene later but does not remind us of judgment now.

As always the church is faced with a great challenge in this latter third of the twentieth century. But one suspects evangelicals will never get out of the starting gate if they ignore the real issues, the real obscenities, while concentrating on the wickedness of nude figures and other things that by comparison are really trivial.

QUESTIONS FOR DISCUSSION

1. Do you agree that obscenity is much more than sexual stimuli?
2. Why do the masses of people tend to think only of sexual stimuli when they hear or use the word "obscenity"?
3. What is meant by the objectification and dehumanization of people?

4. What is meant by the statement "obscenity is a function of context?"
5. Do you agree that blasphemy is more one's condition of heart and life than a certain choice of words?
6. Is the word "nigger" obscene?
7. How do euphemisms distort reality and affect our attitudes toward other people and ideas?
8. Why is the integrity and purity of language one of the chief casualties of war?
9. Do you agree that human language as well as people can be debased and exploited for selfish purposes?
10. Why do you think there is more explicit violence in the movies today than ever before in the history of the motion picture industry?
11. What does more educating of our children—the schools or television?
12. What do you think viewing scene after scene of violence will do to a child?
13. One writer has called the Vietnamese War "the living room war." Should explicit films of war action be shown on the evening news?
14. Do you agree with the author that "the depths of decadence of a nation or society cannot be measured by such a short measuring rod as sexual explicitness"?

9

The Church's Task

Having explored the problem of obscenity and pornography and having attempted to place it in Christian perspective, I am tempted to close the study. Knowing the thinking patterns of many of my brethren, however, I shall be charged with being "soft" on pornography and an advocate of a do-nothing stance. At this point I will say nothing to refute such a charge. But while it is true that of necessity the governmental role in regulating morality in the media is highly restricted, there is an even greater opportunity for institutions and individuals to exert controls according to their particular needs and tastes.

I conclude by offering briefly seven suggestions for church action. Not all of these are of equal value; most are helpful at the local congregational level, but others may be better applied in cooperative efforts among churches in a community or larger affiliation.

EXERCISE VISION IN CONTROL

1. Each church should direct its collective energies in channels that will bring the greatest glory to God and the most help to church members and fellow citizens.

In the past church members who fought pornography

have come off firmly identified with prim little old ladies, country bumpkins, cultural yahoos, radical conservatism, and unadulterated Puritanism. (Of course in actual usage a "Puritan" is anyone whose views of sex are less permissive than your own.) Sometimes churchgoers have flown off at the wrong things. In Vancouver, British Columbia, for example, Indian artist Simon Charlie wood carved a nine-foot high statue of a man to stand in front of the municipal building. The statue was a replica of those used as lodgepoles in Indian villages to welcome visitors and was clothed in a cape and hat. As might be guessed, a local minister complained the statue "violated Christian principles of morality and decency" and rounded up forty signatures from church members requesting that he add a fig leaf. The Indian artist complained that he didn't know what a fig leaf looked like. "Besides, there just aren't any fig leaves on any Indian carvings."[1]

When astronomers Frank Drake and Carl Sagan conceived the idea of attaching a drawing of a nude man and woman to the Pioneer 10 spacecraft, their motive was purely scientific. They wanted any extraterrestrial beings who might some day intercept the craft to know what kind of race had sent it. Since the launch in March, 1972, the drawing has stirred up more controversy on earth than a conceivable first discovery in space.[2] Not unexpectedly, people complained about the morality of the whole drawing. Some newspaper editors censored the picture, erasing the male genitalia and the female nipples. One irate moralist wrote the *Los Angeles Times* and expressed indignation that pornography was bad

1. *Nashville Tennessean*, June 8, 1972.
2. *Time*, June 5, 1972, p. 60.

enough here and "isn't it bad enough that our own space-agency officials have found it necessary to spread this filth even beyond our own solar system."

In March, 1972, the African Heritage Dancers appeared in our city and presented a lively and moving show that was a positive statement about African culture. In this culture the exposure of parts of the body intimately associated with the procreation of life and the nourishment of life has been a valid expression of human emotion at times of crisis and disaster when the life cycle is threatened as in the case of battle. So when the dancers appeared bare-breasted for a number which was considered tasteful by a large high school student body and faculty, it was only a matter of a day or two before parents and administrators united in condemnation. These critics were "respectable" Christians, they claimed. They may have filtered out the evidence in the Old Testament of a Hebrew practice of rending garments to expose the body in the face of disasters or the prophetic practice of occasionally appearing naked in public at times of national crisis. Nor had it dawned on them that it just might be healthier for an African wife to expose her breast during a warrior dance to express her life commitment to her husband as he enters battle than for American women to expose all (or at least most) of theirs for selling magazines, movie admissions, liquor, autos, and cigars.

When Christians engage in such petition signing or letter writing campaigns wherein censorship is so pointless, so absurd, they only bring disrespect upon the church and the Christian life. Further, pointless censorship or protest only causes confusion among our young people who are in the process of developing adult attitudes toward the human body.

We run into the same kind of problem with boycotting or picketing of stores that sell pornography. This only calls the attention of the impressionable to the fact that the store is around and where it is located. If church leadership is concerned with establishing priorities, the call for picketing and boycotting should be shunned. The myopia of chasing pornography on 42nd Street, Broad Street, Peachtree Street, Sunset Boulevard, or Woodward Avenue may prevent the laity from seeing the real obscenities in life, a point discussed in the previous chapter. But it is interesting to note that, according to a University of Chicago poll of noted psychologists and psychiatrists, "a thumping 86.1% said they thought that the people who vigorously try to suppress pornography were in many cases motivated by unresolved sexual problems of their own."[3] Further, the Christian wants to avoid coercion; his desire is not to *force* his standards on an unbelieving world.

What about the value of affiliation with such watchdog organizations as "Morality in Media" or "Citizens for Decent Literature"? While one may appreciate the motive behind these organizations and the obvious sincerity of many who channel their energies through these groups, the Christian should be highly suspicious. First, in some cases these self-appointed guardians of public morality have exploited plain stupidity and fear about sex education to build up the organization. Second, some of their goals are questionable, the most pernicious being the effort to remove the socially redeeming value test from state obscenity laws. Third, the amount of money amassed for the battle may be far out of proportion to the problem at hand. *Saturday Review*

3. Reported in *Publisher's Weekly*, September 29, 1969, p. 43.

reports in an editorial that "Morality in Media's" three-year fund raising plan aimed at a whopping $2,049,700; if this is reached the organization would be spending about fourteen cents for every six cents in profit taken by hard-core producers.[4]

As should be clear from this study, the ample amount of pornography in our society is a symptom of the sexual sickness that abounds—not the cause of it. And within the church which teaches sexual morality on the basis of fear (detection, infection, conception), there may be a tendency to strike out at pornography as though it were the problem rather than simply a confirmation of a malaise much deeper. If our righteous indignation is channeled into mobilizing adult members into "porn squads" to check on stores and offer "seals of approval," petitioning and letter writing campaigns, boycotting, and other forms of pressure action, our efforts may bear little fruit simply because these are attempts to cure a disease by eliminating the symptoms. The effect is like that of dealing with an itching sore. Long and painful treatment is necessary for healing but it feels so good to scratch it and bring temporary relief; of course the sore may be further aggravated.

Instead of spending our time and energies in Bible classes and individual study and research condemning pornography consumers, it would be far better to understand why men crave vicarious, frustrating, and ultimately isolating erotic experiences. What message from man is revealed in the language of pornography? Is it telling us we have a double standard? Does it tell us the young disdain traditional values and taboos? What does

---

4. Editorial by Kenneth D. McCormick and W. L. Smith, *Saturday Review,* July 22, 1972, pp. 24-25.

it tell of the sexual frustrations and encounters of those who prey upon it? How can the church respond to their needs? How can the quality of family life be enhanced? Underlying the appetite for indecency, is there a genuine quest for meaning and purpose in sex? Wherein were the failures? How can the causes be eliminated?

PATRONIZE THE ARTS

2. The church should encourage young artists in their midst and the endeavors of artists in general.

Too often Christians have viewed art as a hobby for the intellectual elite or an elective course in a college curriculum. Such a relegation does not do the artist justice. But the artist in modern history has long been accustomed to the indifference and, quite frequently, the condemnation of church leaders. Religious leaders have often exhibited rigidity, narrowness, and low aesthetic standards when it came to evaluating the arts. Rather than a sensitive probing and listening to what the great works of art had to say, energy was exerted in polemics aimed at getting church members to distrust and reject the artists and their contributions. To this day the hostility between the artists' community and many conservative and fundamentalist churches continues almost unabated. Part of it may be traced to the Puritan philosophy that what man finds pleasurable and physically gratifying is automatically and inherently suspect as detrimental to spiritual welfare. Further, many church members have simply misinterpreted the intentions of artists and failed to see the intrinsic value of their creativity. But much of the tension between artists and conservative Christians is rooted in the historical

tradition of an anti-sensual (or anti-life) theology and an
excessive emphasis on "other-worldliness."

Art has a revelatory function. It tells something of
the often overlooked qualities of life and the world. It
reinvigorates man's perceptions of other men and wom-
en, the environment, the earth and other aspects of
reality that are often filtered out by the habitual or
prejudiced eye and ear. "If the theologian remains aloof
from the work of artists," asserts John P. Newport, "he
is ignoring the world which theology attempts to understand in relation to God."[5] Art gives us new options. As
Albert Camus stated shortly before the Nobel ceremony
in 1957: "There is not a single true work of art that has
not in the end added to the inner freedom of each
person who has known and loved it."[6]

To borrow theological jargon, the artist plays the
roles of both priest and prophet. As priest, the artist
expresses the voices, dreams, disappointments, values,
and general culture of the society of which he is a part.
Art is an ordering of human existence. The artist re-
duces the chaos around him to intelligible order until
experience assumes a shape that can be grasped and
understood in a larger community. He mirrors our age in
such a way that when future historians want to understand our civilization they will look not only to our
wars and politics; they will read our books, see our
paintings, architecture, sculpture and, if possible, our
films. Thus, to grasp the *zeitgeist*, the theologian or
other serious thinker must consult the artists; in a
unique way they document the time-spirit.

5. John P. Newport, *Theology and Contemporary Art Forms*
(Waco, Texas: Word Books, 1971), p. 14.
6. Albert Camus, *Resistance, Rebellion, and Death* (New York:
Alfred A. Knopf, Inc., 1960), p. 241.

Not only do artists mirror and preserve an epoch, but in a prophetic role they offer criticism and direction. And like the Old Testament prophet, the artist may want to condemn with an element of compassion. If his efforts call us to action, the revelatory work becomes a transforming work. How often has a new perception of a person of another nation, another race, or of the opposite sex radically changed our attitudes and actions? The artist as prophet enlarges our perceptual field in terms of reality as he subjectively sees it. Roger L. Shinn has correctly summarized the distinction between art and religion:

> Christianity in particular is the faith of a community with a mission of healing, reconciling, and proclaiming the gospel. This mission constitutes its unique prophetic-priestly vocation.
>
> Art, like religion, may be naturalistic, skeptical, Christian, or heretical. Christian faith will, therefore, sometimes meet attack or support in art. But it will welcome the revelatory insight of all high art. Even the artist who scorns the church will, insofar as he explores and enriches the experience of mankind, serve God.[7]

The church must get a message across to the artist. An artist must exercise complete freedom in dealing with human society. No human idea, emotion, or action

---

7. Finley Eversole (ed.) *Christian Faith and the Contemporary Arts* (Nashville: Abingdon Press, 1962), p. 79. Used by permission of publisher. This book is must reading on this topic. It contains several illustrations and has a helpful bibliography for further reading.

can be forbidden to him. His commitment must be to truth, not commercial gain. Truth is the highest and noblest form of artistic commitment, just as it is the highest form of moral commitment, annoying or disgusting as it may be to the would-be censor or average citizen. The church must convince the artist that his vision is welcome. It must impress upon him that his talen is a gift from God and that it should not be prostituted by commercial gimmickry or exploitation. To whom much is given, much is required.

Some of the most meaningful ideas on the relationship of a Christian artist to his creative activity may be found in the writings of Catholic novelist Flannery O'Connor.[8] A few of these ideas are worth mentioning here. O'Connor states that the first duty of the novelist (and this applies to all artists) is to open his eyes on the world about him and observe. "If what he sees is not highly edifying, he is still required to look. Then he is required to reproduce, with words, what he sees."[9] She acknowledges the fact that many Christian artists are involved in writing (or painting, filming, etc.) in order to use the finished product in support and proof of the faith, or at least to prove the existence of a Divine Being. To her, these are "low motives." She acknowledges that we often see people busily distorting talents in order to enhance their popularity or fill their pocketbooks. If this is done consciously, it is reprehensible. She sees pornography as "essentially sentimental, for it leaves out the connection of sex with its hard purpose,

---

8. See Flannery O'Connor, *Mystery and Manners,* selected and edited by Sally and Robert Fitzgerald (New York: Farrar, Straus, and Giroux, 1969). All quotes from this volume are used by permission of publisher.
9. *Ibid.,* p. 177.

and so far disconnects it from its meaning in life as to make it simply an experience for its own sake."[10] But even more frequently, she believes, artists distort their talents in the name of God for motivations they deem noble—teaching, reforming, or making converts for the church. She admits that "it is much less easy to say that this is reprehensible."[11] And she goes on to say:

> None of us is able to judge such people themselves, but we must, for the sake of truth, judge the products they make. We must say whether this or that novel truthfully portrays the aspect of reality that it sets out to portray. The novelist who deliberately misuses his talent for some good purpose may be committing no sin, but he is certainly committing a grave inconsistency, for he is trying to reflect God with what amounts to a practical untruth.[12]

The serious artist is always concerned with the flaw in human nature. This is his beginning point. "Drama usually bases itself on the bedrock of original sin, whether the writer thinks in theological terms or not."[13] In a vivid and often disrupting way the arts focus on the vital issues and themes which are the central concern of theology. For example, the novelist writes about characters in a world where something is obviously lacking, where the general mystery of incompleteness and the particular tragedy of our own times is apparent. Dealing with such vital issues, the artist takes his work seriously

---

10. *Ibid.*, p. 148.
11. *Ibid.*, pp. 173-74.
12. *Ibid.*
13. *Ibid.*, p. 167.

and keeps in mind that "we reflect the church in everything that we do, and those who can see clearly that our judgment is false in matters of art cannot be blamed for suspecting our judgment in matters of religion."[14] In one of the great lines from her essays, O'Connor states that "When people have told me that because I am a Catholic, I cannot be an artist, I have had to reply, ruefully, that because I am a Catholic, I cannot afford to be less than artist."[15]

The church should publicize the efforts of local Christian artists. Where there are public performances they should be publicized in church announcements and publications. The educational program of the church should consider incorporating the use of drama, essays, and even novels in communicating the Christian message.

Most larger churches have a church library. The staid shelves of these libraries sometimes contain little else but 75-year-old commentaries valuable only because they are some of the few extant copies of some now-defunct sectarian press. Or, there may be a few "religious novels" gathering dust on the shelves since their superficial and unreal characters who are engaged in stock situations render them undistinguished. These should be moved over to make room for new volumes reflecting what the best historians, biographers, and novelists have to offer. Some of the more relevant volumes can be publicized in the church bulletin and employed by Sunday School teachers in showing their distinctive message to contemporary Christianity. Church leaders should be alert to other programs geared to encourage church members to read good books and patronize the other arts.

---

14. *Ibid.*, p. 190.
15. *Ibid.*, p. 146.

OFFER GUIDELINES FOR PRIVATE DECISION-MAKING

3. Church media, primarily periodical publications, should offer more reviews and guidelines for individual choice in the entertainment media.

Now obviously this is already being done in the major denominations. In many of the conservative and fundamentalist groups there is very little if any serious effort made to help individual Christians make meaningful choices in recreation and entertainment.

Because of their immense popularity with young adults, movies should be given careful, critical review. An intelligent reviewer will acknowledge that all artistic and worthwhile films (and plays and books, for that matter) can be relevant to the Christian perspective on what it means to be a human. All films are "message" films. Each molds thought and action patterns. Many films, of course, do not have a very good message; their method is escape from reality.

Several years ago Malcolm Boyd developed this idea and carried it a step further; to him, all films are "theological." "A creative person may simply write a book or screen play about people and things; he has no realized Christian concept at all, indeed he may deny the existence of God," says Boyd. "Yet such a writer's finished product is of intense interest to us because without knowing it, he is dealing with God, with evil, with sin, with Incarnation and Atonement."[16]

A number of film producers and directors likely imagined themselves doing the church real service by turning

---

16. Malcolm Boyd, "All Films are Theological," *Christian Century*, December 1, 1954, p. 1456.

out "beards and bathrobes"-type religious epics costing millions to finance. This type of pseudo-biblical extravaganza is not so popular these days and, as far as Christian service goes, it is just as well. The more creative, the more enriching, and more relevant artistic efforts are frequently done by novelists, playwrights, and screen-writers who instruct us without intending to. Mike Nichols' *The Graduate*, very popular with young people, portrayed vividly the futility of sexual experience without personal involvement.[17] I have a minister friend who temporarily was ostracized from the mainstream of the fellowship he serves, not because he endorsed *Midnight Cowboy*, but because he acknowledged there was a powerful message there. The opposition and fear of his congregation to the realistic language and explicit sex (I doubt they were disturbed by the explicit violence) did not change the truth of that message: in this land of ours there is much degradation, sin, and alienation but in a rather unusual situation, God is immanently at work bringing people together in unaffected bonds of friendship.

So the question for Christian reviewers must not be, "Is this a Christian film?" or "Is this a religious film?" but rather, "As a Christian concerned about a sinful world being reconciled to a loving God, what relevance, what message, does this film have for me?" The entertainment media does not "owe" the churches anything. We must not expect the movie industry to serve the institutional or spiritual interests of organized religion any more than the interests or concerns of the political and business world. No medium should be the organ for

---

17. For a theological critique of this film, see Herbert W. Richardson, *Nun, Witch and Playmate: The Americanization of Sex* (New York: Harper and Row, 1972), pp. 118-25.

party propaganda. Its role is to entertain and enlighten man's intellect, spirit, and conscience by fulfilling its highest potential as a unique art form. Morality and art are related. And, in the words of Paul Lehman, "the degree to which the film fails as an artistic achievement is the degree to which it also fails as a moral achievement."[18]

In individual decision-making, and in critical reviews of films, plays, and books, how are questionable materials to be handled? What criteria should be used in the rating system? Reviewers must never look to a set of rules of thumb or inflexible criteria for guidance. The quantity of skin shown, the depth of cleavage, the amount of verbal obscenity, demonstration of results of godless immorality or lack of same—such canons utilized unbendingly are the way of foolishness. "Is it shocking? Is it disgusting?" answered affirmatively is not reason for automatic rejection.

"Each film must be examined in light of what it says about and to the human condition as the Christian community knows that situation to be revealed in Jesus Christ," suggests editor, minister, and critic James M. Wall. "Acknowledging that each generation arrives at varying specifics in regard to treatment of the human equation, we can nevertheless watch for the extent to which man's situation is authentically delineated on the screen."[19]

One thing evangelical Christians especially need to

18. Paul Lehman, "A Christian Look at the Sexual Revolution," *Sexual Ethics and Christian Responsibility*, ed. John Charles Wynn (New York: Association Press, 1970), p. 59.
19. James M. Wall, "Toward a Christian Film Criteria," *Christian Century*, June 12, 1965, pp. 776-77. See also Robert Tracy, "Literature and Obscenity," *Christian Century*, June 12, 1965, p. 771.

guard against is imposition of their standards of entertainment upon all others. And certainly we should take
heed not to censure another for attending a controversial movie (I exclude those obviously pornographic, exploitation films and refer to, say, an R-rated movie)
when we have not seen it for ourselves. True, a movie or
play may be wholly unsuitable for children and, consequently, some adults may be ill-equipped to see the
production. But it is one of the privileges of adulthood
in a free society to expose oneself to the depiction of
life and make one's own interpretation. The church's
task is not to deprive adults of this experience, either by
dictate or subtle insinuation. Rather the teaching ministry of the church should provide adults with the proper
criteria of interpretation and to supply in-depth answers
to serious questions.[20] The words of Jesus seem so
apropós here: "Judge not, that ye be not judged."[21]

PROVIDE FOR WHOLESOMENESS IN LEISURE

4. Churches and church-related schools should provide wholesome recreation and entertainment for youth.

---

20. For further study in this area some recent books have been
published. The following are recommended as useful in pro-
viding criteria for decision-making and evaluation: Neil P.
Hurley, *Theology Through Film* (New York: Harper and
Row, 1970); Bruce Knox, *The World of Film* (Richmond,
Virginia: John Knox, 1972) gets into the debate over sex and
violence; Murray Schumach, *The Face of the Cutting Room
Floor* (New York: William Morrow and Co., 1964); Robert G.
Konzelman, *Marquee Ministry: The Movie Theatre as Church
and Community Forum* (New York: Harper and Row, 1972);
James M. Wall, *Church and Cinema: A Way of Viewing Film*
(Grand Rapids, Michigan: Eerdmans Publishing Company,
1971); G. William Jones, *Sunday Night at the Movies* (Richmond, Virginia: John Knox Press, 1967).
21. Matthew 7:1.

Again, here is a suggestion that is already utilized by most religious groups. The only question is whether it is given the proper emphasis. Wholesome recreation and entertainment is necessary for young people to develop healthy interpersonal relations. With a little creativity church building facilities, including and especially the parking lot, can be convertible into recreational and entertainment areas.

Christian colleges could, in watching a budget that must necessarily be trimmed of fat, cut other services and facilities *before* physical education and recreational facilities, good films, artist series, and the like. For schools still operating under the philosophy of *in loco parentis*, the drafting of student handbooks for behavior codes should avoid excessive emphasis on the non-moral aspects of student behavior and dress, and direct more attention to the kind of curricula and campus atmosphere that creates genuinely concerned, intelligent, and involved graduates—graduates who can place all the moral crises that they will soon be facing into the proper Christian perspective.

It is important that the same facilities and opportunities be open to older people as well, very often the most neglected people in the church.

SUPPLEMENT SEX EDUCATION

5. The church should take a more active role in the sex education of young adults.

Because parents are often ill-equipped or too reticent to be effective, and with the public school's piecemeal and uneven approach, the church should fill the gap. Sound and thorough sex education is probably the best informal control of pornography with young people.

When a young person perceives a deficiency in his knowledge of sex, he may turn to pornography or at best unreliable sources to fill the vacuum.

For an age often lauded for its enlightenment and openness about sex, it is amazing how little accurate information even college level church members have about human sexuality. Many college-age Christians have a thirst for factual information and positive attitudes toward sex. A frank discussion of the sexual union which emphasizes the beauty of its procreative, communicative, and aesthetic dimensions is readily received by them. But the approach must be objective, unembarrassed, and mature. A teaching colleague of mine in clinical psychology, Dr. Robert Sturgeon, insists that the attitude conveyed in sex education is, perhaps, more important than even the information itself. Well-intentioned but untrained Christian educators often teach embarrassment, disgust, frustration, or rejection by their approach. Once sex is learned as a "dirty" thing, this view does not magically and suddenly disappear because a wedding service has been performed; in fact, the attitude may persist for the rest of one's life and we have probably all met people with such attitudes. The local congregation, then, can lead honest and open dialogue on human sexuality, beginning early in life and continuing into young adulthood, and create positive, healthy attitudes and thus reduce the possibility of sexual hang-ups.

The denominational bodies that have not as yet devised a fellowship-wide curriculum should consider doing so. There are many excellent films and other group teaching aids that are already available for leasing.

Should public school sex education become more uniformly effective this would be no call for the churches to vacate the area. For what better atmosphere is there for learning that sexual knowledge and moral responsibility go hand-in-hand?

MINISTER TO SPECIAL NEEDS

6. The church should minister competently and compassionately to individuals who have sex problems.

The church or synagogue must be a caring community that is concerned about people at all ages and stages of life. If religious ministry is to be relevant to the needs of individuals, families, and communities, we must never forget that mental and spiritual health are interrelated. One cannot arbitrarily separate his relationships with self and others (mental health) from his relationship with God, the universe, and ultimate values (spiritual health). Positive mental health is included in the biblical term "wholeness" and no conception of spiritual health is complete if it ignores mental health. Both kinds of health are directed toward the fulfillment of human potentialities for living a constructive life in mutually gratifying, loving relationships.

A personal crisis or obsession is not unusual; in fact, it might be expected sometime during the lives of all of us. There may be several people within each congregation who are encountering difficulty in establishing meaningful interpersonal relations. The supportive fellowship of the entire congregation must be maintained at all times. In many congregations the threat of "withdrawing fellowship" from those persisting in sin (an act restored from primitive Christianity) rings hollow in the ears of those we are disciplining. The reason is simple— we have never fully extended the kind of fellowship that was practiced in the first and second generations of the church and there is literally nothing to withdraw. If the kind of fellowship practiced in New Testament times were practiced by contemporary churches, many of the personal problems and hang-ups of Christians within this fellowship would have no opportunity for development.

It must be stressed that problems and sins of a sexual nature are no more serious or sinful than are problems or sins of other types. But very often our attitudes toward the sinner entrapped in a sexual situation create an unnecessary barrier in our attempts to help and restore him to a better life. Such an attitude is not new. This attitude is easily seen in the self-righteous Pharisees who brought the woman caught in the act of adultery to Jesus. Why is it much easier for many church members to accept again into full fellowship the one who has offended, gossiped, lied, neglected his family, or stolen, than the one who has a sexual hang-up or has behaved irresponsibly? Perhaps too many have not come to grips with their own sexuality, with their own problems and motives and frustrations. Until we are able to face and deal with our own sexual problems and fears it will continue to be a challenge for us to assist anyone else in similar circumstances without belittling him. Guilt, difficulty in discussing matters of a sexual nature, and the fear of being humiliated and even condemned, have frequently converged to make it extremely painful if not impossible for many to seek help from a Christian person. If we are serious about making the church a caring community that reaches out to all people in all kinds of human situations, we must act to eradicate negative and self-righteous attitudes and double standards that are so subtly communicated, and establish such interpersonal relations that when a problem arises, the Christian friend is the *first* one to be sought for advice. Such a fellowship can help a person move from guilt to reconciliation employing the time tested pathway of confrontation, confession, forgiveness, restitution, and reconciliation (restoration of severed relationships).

An awareness of the needs of special groups—the older unmarried men and women, the younger widowed, the younger unmarried adults, parents without partners, etc.—is essential to a closely knit and servant congregation. Not only is the church concerned with reconciliation but with primary prevention of problems. Since no person is able to maintain his existence solely by himself, the local congregation is in a particularly strategic position to provide group activities that offer intimacy, support, and relationship. This nurturing of man's emotional needs through interpersonal relationships is a necessary part of maintaining meaningful and wholesome existence. The social programming a church's leadership provides to fulfill this normal and necessary function need not have any overtly spiritual orientation to justify its value. Neither should such groups be therapy experiences, or supervised by professional psychologists and psychiatrists. The opportunity they provide for human communication and relationship to people who are relatively isolated and need structured means of participating in human relationships provides self-justification for such a program.

Above and beyond this there needs to be greater emphasis on competent pastoral counseling so that the less socially understood and accepted forms of sexual deviance may be handled competently and responsibly. In the 1960's a number of denominational leaders began

202 / OBSCENITY, PORNOGRAPHY, AND CENSORSHIP

to realize this need so that today, in most accredited
seminaries and theological schools, one can major in this
special form of ministry.[22]

INDIVIDUAL RESPONSIBILITY

7. Each individual Christian must assume a large measure of responsibility in decision-making for himself and
his family.

A Christian father, for example, should not expect
the church or another institution to be the ultimate
guardian of his family's morals when very clearly the
Bible teaches that the responsibility is his.[23] The sad
truth is that so many parents are ill-equipped to dis-
charge their responsibilities. And when things go wrong
the human tendency is to look outside the family (to
the media, the schools, associates, etc.) to find a scapegoat for our failures.

On an individual level, each consumer has the "good
old" democratic right to choose not to buy a product,
see a movie, or read a magazine if he thinks its patron-
age will encourage indecency. Collective individual consumer action has worked effectively in many other
areas. After all, producers and manufacturers only give
the public what they want and only so long as they
want it.

Individual parents must have full control in the privacy of their homes. Parental capitulation to children's

---

22. There are several books in the area of pastoral counseling
which are very helpful. One which is recommended is Howard
J. Clinebell, Jr. (ed.), *Community Mental Health: The Role of
Church and Temple* (Nashville: Abingdon Press, 1970). It
contains several brief reading lists for additional study.
23. Ephesians 6:4.

wishes in television programming is irresponsible. It is also ironic. If some demented teen-ager who could not do anything but tell sex and violence yarns were hanging around the neighborhood, few parents would allow their preschoolers up to forty hours a week with him. He would be called a menace. But why the equanimity about children's experience with the "boob tube"?

Older children can handle almost any perception if they have someone to guide their response or reaction. Television's role in showing astronauts cruising in a buggy across the surface of the moon, describing other cultures or the animal world, showing the birth of a baby, or relating a great historical event have all enriched beyond measure the intellectual and cultural environment of children. But when parents believe it is bringing premature awareness of genuine evil, family censorship can be effected by turning the channel knob. Parents can read reviews in advance and select programs or, better yet, coview these shows with children. Commercials can be made a learning experience by asking children to analyze them and offer their insight into what they think the sponsors were doing to motivate them to buy the product or service; their insight might surprise you.

As Christians we need not bemoan the fact that the media are basically a consumer delivery system. But we must do all within our ability to raise our tastes and keep aloft our values so that there will be a natural insistence that the media deliver only that which is authentically honest, relevant, and enriching to the character of man.

The Christian home is the best place for a discussion of contemporary novels, plays, and movies. If a high school or college student in the home has a reading assignment in some biography or novel, why shouldn't the parents share that reading and discuss the situations presented in the light of Christian principles? This would have the added benefit of revealing to our children that we are interested in their general activities and education.

EPILOGUE

A final statement. It may seem as though this book has applied more to the needs and interests of young adults than to any other group. Let it be! After all, youth attend more movies and plays, read more books, magazines, and journals, and give more substantive support to the arts. This is good. But their life style troubles their parents' generation. It has always been popular to believe that the young people are "going to the dogs," but the belief now is that somehow this generation just has to be more immoral, more rebellious toward authority, and more disrespectful of bequeathed attitudes. A cardinal piece of evidence ushered forth in support of this theory is the young generation's acceptance of new standards of morality in the media and, more inclusively, of interpersonal relations altogether.

As for myself, I believe this whole issue should be seen in context. I find much to applaud wildly in young people today—their intolerance with racial injustice, their courageous questioning of a senseless war, their interest in preserving our environment, their demand that we re-order national priorities, their decreasing emphasis on material goods, and more emphasis on honest interpersonal relations and social improvement. But the tension of these reforms and the tension of the new freedom in sex can lead to frustration and disillusionment.

I appeal to the whole institutional church to open its doors and minds to these our younger brothers and sisters to show the relevance of Christianity to all of man's problems, and to give moral direction to the enormous talents and energies of these young people in the service of all humanity. This policy just might mean the survival of the prophetic community and, in turn, the establishment of a just and humane society.

QUESTIONS FOR DISCUSSION

1. Why have Christian people fighting pornography often come across as narrow-minded "do-gooders"?
2. Should Christians organize pressure groups or boycotts to fight establishments that sell unappreciated publications?
3. How is pornography more of a symptom of sexual sickness than a cause of it?
4. Why have conservative and funadamentalist churches been unappreciative of, even hostile to, the artists' community?
5. How does the artist serve the church?
6. How can the local congregation support the efforts of young Christian artists?
7. Should church libraries contain more than only religious books?
8. Do you agree that all artistic and worthwhile films can be relevant to the Christian perspective on the meaning of human existence?
9. How do some artists perform a service for the church without intending to?
10. What films have you seen which were not directly religious in nature but you felt were worthwhile in teaching you more about life and human relations?
11. Why is the expenditure of funds from the church budget for recreation facilities and services justified?
12. Is the attitude conveyed in sex education more important than the content itself?
13. Are sins of a sexual nature more serious or sinful than

shortcomings of other types? If not, how do you explain that such sins have often aroused our ire and indignation more than other kinds of problems?

14. Do you think parents today exercise enough control over their children's television viewing habits?